Qi Gong For Beginners

Qi Gong

For Beginners

Eight Easy Movements for Vibrant Health

Stanley D. Wilson, Ph.D.

Photography by Barry Kaplan

Rudra Press
Portland, Oregon

Rudra Press
PO Box 13390
Portland, Oregon 97213
Telephone: 503-235-0175
Telefax: 503-235-0909

This book is not intended to replace expert medical advice. The author and publisher urge you to verify the appropriateness of any exercise with your qualified health care professional. The author and publisher disclaim any liability or loss, personal or otherwise, resulting from the information in this book.

Art Direction, book design and typography by Bill Stanton
Photography by Barry Kaplan

Library of Congress Cataloging-in-Publication Data

Wilson, Stanley D., 1944 -
        Qi gong for beginners : eight easy movements for vibrant health /
    Stanley D. Wilson : photography by Barry Kaplan.
            p.   cm.
            Includes bibliographical references.
            ISBN 0-915801-75-2
            1. Ch' i kung   I. Title.
    RA781.8.W55   1997
    613.7' 1—dc21

To Debrah and Noelle,
beloved wife and daughter

contents

acknowledgments

Qi Gong For Beginners required a great deal of support and teamwork which came through the efforts of the following people.

I am grateful to Iona Marsaa Teeguarden, a gifted healer and teacher, for introducing me to the simple but powerful movements of Pal Dan Gum.

A deep bow to Karen Kreiger, the President of Rudra Press, for believing in this project from the beginning and for many helpful suggestions along the way. Her sustained enthusiasm, professionalism, and commitment to excellence have made the entire publishing process an unexpected delight.

Much appreciation to Gloria Balcom, MicroSly Marketing consultant, for placing my original manuscript in the hands of Karen Kreiger. It is impossible to over-emphasize the importance of finding the right publisher and I have Gloria to thank for finding the people at Rudra Press.

I am especially grateful to Ellen Hynson, Managing Editor at Rudra Press, for taking my original manuscript and crafting it into a better organized and more readable book.

To Bill Stanton for his skillful direction of the artwork, and for his design and layout that have made *Qi Gong for Beginners* so elegant and attractive.

I want to thank Barry Kaplan for his excellent photography. I believe he has captured the essence of Pal Dan Gum; in large part it is his skillful photography that distinguishes this book from others on Qi Gong.

Thank you Robin Mesch for a wonderful job modeling the Eight Silken Movements. It is said the earliest Qi Gong methods were patterned after animal-like movements and Robin embodies those most valued—grace, flexibility, strength, and extraordinary balance.

To Barbara Lee, stylist, for her important contribution to the success of the photography in this book, and for her positive energy at the photo session.

I would like to express heartfelt gratitude to Debrah Wilson, my beloved wife of sixteen years, for always being there with support and encouragement when I need it most.

To Noelle Wilson, my lovely teenage daughter, for opening my heart and inspiring me to follow a spiritual path. May you live a life of harmony, inner balance, and spiritual well-being.

To my sister Dianne Nicholson, grammarian extraordinaire, for proofreading my manuscript and making a number of constructive suggestions. Dianne, you should seriously consider a second career as a book editor!

To Lorin Wilson, my father, for supporting my loftiest goals, and for not only encouraging me to follow the path of service, but making it possible.

To Yvonne Lovejoy, my mother, for modeling empathy and compassion, and for instilling in me a belief that intention can move mountains.

To Darlene McGlocklin, younger sister and fitness guru, for the important part she has played in my healing and in my life.

To Michael Gladych, raja yoga master, enlightened elder, and good friend, for teaching me the essence of self-healing, namely, balanced energy that restores the body's genetic memory of wellness.

I want to thank Dave Borg and Claudia Cheyne, two friends who successfully negotiate the perils of spiritual life, for generously loaning me books and materials from their Qi Gong library.

Thank you Tereasa Burgess for your excellent artwork.

To Nanette Howard for helping type the manuscript, showing me how to properly format the text, and getting things done on time.

...make the impossible possible, the possible easy, and the easy elegant.
—MOSHE FELDENKRAIS

Knowing the ancient beginning is the essence of Tao.
   —LAO TZU
    Tao Te Ching (14)

*In the pursuit of learning, every day something is acquired. In the pursuit of
Tao, every day something is dropped.*
   —LAO TZU
    Tao Te Ching (48)

> *Qi Gong* (chee kung): 1) An ancient Oriental method of building and bal-
> ancing life energy through exercise. 2) A general name for many different
> sets of exercises that emphasize the role of movement, proper breathing, and
> concentration.

In 1979 I developed an interest in shiatsu, or acupressure, a form of thera-
peutic finger pressure applied to areas and points of the body treated by
acupuncture. I took a class taught by Iona Marsaa Teeguarden at the
Acupressure Workshop in Santa Monica, California in order to learn the theory and technique of Jin Shin Do® ("The Way of the Compassionate Spirit"),
an acupressure therapy originated and developed by Iona, integrating
acupuncture theory and Reichian principles, along with "Taoist yoga." My
intention was to integrate acupressure principles and Reichian body therapy
to facilitate a deeper release of the chronic armor-like muscular tensions I
treated daily in my psychology practice. Iona had studied in Japan and with
numerous masters of the oriental healing arts in America and was clearly a
gifted healer. As it turned out, her greatest gift to me was not the acupressure
technique, but a meditation-in-motion that originated in the Orient approximately two thousand years ago.

One evening, after an all-day session of instruction and practice, Iona showed us how to do a sequence of simple but powerful exercises that reminded me of Tài Chi Chuan (commonly known as Tài Chi), but were infinitely easier to learn. She called these exercises Pal Dan Gum, which translated from Korean means Eight Silken Movements (note: In this book I most often make reference to Pal Dan Gum rather than its English translation, Eight Silken Movements, or Eight Easy Movements, as it is sometimes refferred to).

As I began mirroring Iona's movements and stretches, I was feeling exhausted and irritable, but after only six minutes I became remarkably relaxed and energized. I was surprised at the sudden and dramatic change in how I felt, physically and emotionally, and wondered what had happened. I realized that Pal Dan Gum was nothing less than extraordinary, and I began a daily practice which I continue to this day.

Having previously learned Tài Chi, I was already familiar with the ancient practice of using energy exercises to promote health and longevity. I enjoyed the gentle slowness and gracefulness of Tài Chi, but I found that I much preferred Pal Dan Gum, not only because it was easier to learn, but because the movements seemed more dynamic and energizing. Iona was an excellent teacher who gave me precise instruction. I arranged for her to teach a class in Pal Dan Gum and acupressure to doctors, nurses, and physical therapists at the hospital where I worked.

We teach what we want to learn, and I wanted to master Pal Dan Gum. I decided to write a book giving clear directions and enough instructional photographs to make the sequence of movements understandable and easy to learn. In the eighteen years since I learned Pal Dan Gum, I have performed the entire sequence of movements well over 10,000 times. During those years, I also devoted countless hours to the study of Oriental medical philosophy, Taoist Esoteric Yoga, Indian Raja Yoga, Buddhist psychology, many forms of meditation, alternative forms of healing, and New Age energy medicine. And I have taught Pal Dan Gum to anyone and everyone who expressed an interest in learning the movements—friends, family, patients, other health care professionals, even strangers at the beach who saw me practicing and asked what I was doing.

Actually, Pal Dan Gum is easy to teach, easy to learn, and easy to do. If you don't have the interest or energy to do aerobics, equipment-assisted workouts, or other "no pain, no gain" routines, but want to be more physically fit, you will love Pal Dan Gum. If you prefer a hard workout, Pal Dan Gum is an excellent warm-up to your usual routine. In fact, its emphasis on gentle and safe stretching makes it an ideal warm-up, or cool-down, for almost any athletic activity—swimming, golf, skiing, bowling, weight training, racket sports, or whatever you choose. Pal Dan Gum can be practiced anywhere—at home, at work, or on the road. In China, Korea, and Japan, people of all ages fill the parks and squares each morning to do their favorite form of energy exercise, a tradition the rest of the world would do well to emulate.

Pal Dan Gum is also ideal if you don't have the time or patience to spend many hours trying to learn the more than 100 poses of T'ai Chi, but still want to do a meditation in motion to achieve vibrant health. Nor does it take thirty minutes or more to perform the sequence of movements; Pal Dan Gum takes only six minutes from start to finish! You do not need any special props, special clothing, exercise equipment or workout setting to get started. Chapter 6 gives you clear step-by-step instructions and photographs for each of the Eight Silken Movements. *But, however tempting, please do not skip ahead and begin doing the exercises!* First read the earlier chapters to learn the essential information needed to provide a firm foundation for your practice.

- Chapter 1 explains the fundamental concept of Qi, the vital energy sustaining all life. Qi Gong is explained as an ancient method of building and balancing energy.
- Chapter 2 traces the origins of Pal Dan Gum to the ancient school of medical Qi Gong and compares it to the more familiar T'ai Chi.
- Chapter 3 teaches you a proper breathing pattern, how Pal Dan Gum encourages and conditions such a pattern, and the numerous health benefits that result.
- Chapter 4 discusses the importance of training your body.
- Chapter 5 deals with training your mind.
- Chapter 6 offers practice guidelines and instructs you on executing each movement.
- Chapter 7 gives you several suggestions on refining your practice.
- Chapter 8 defines vibrant health and explains self-healing.
- Chapter 9 teaches you two Qi Gong sitting meditations for health and healing.

A Word of Caution: Pal Dan Gum is a sequence of eight gentle, almost no-impact exercises intended to improve your health. However, like any exercise or stretching program, the movements taught in this book could result in an injury. If you are currently rehabilitating an injury or experiencing any physical pain, please consult your health care professional before beginning to practice. If doing these exercises brings on or worsens a pain condition, stop and get professional help before continuing.

* * * *

Pal Dan Gum has been an integral part of a healing regimen that has allowed me to miraculously recover from a life-threatening illness. While I cannot promise you a miracle, I am convinced you will significantly improve your health and longevity by doing these simple but powerful exercises.

The Eight Silken Movements are designed to improve our physical, emotional, and spiritual well-being by restoring a strong and balanced energy flow throughout the body. When practiced regularly according to the guidelines in this book, you can expect to:

- strengthen the body as a whole
- improve postural alignment and flexibility
- relieve muscular tension and pain
- promote deeper and more efficient respiration
- boost energy levels and stamina
- stimulate the immune system to prevent or heal illness
- activate the relaxation response to reduce stress
- return to your optimal size and shape
- increase sexual arousal and improve sexual functioning
- increase blood circulation and cardiovascular fitness
- improve digestion
- increase youthfulness and longevity
- develop emotional well-being and a positive approach to life
- cultivate concentration, self-awareness, and self-discipline
- lead a more spiritually oriented life

Because I have personally benefited so much from my years of practicing Pal Dan Gum, I passionately believe it should be shared with everyone. By passing it along to others who might also benefit, this book becomes my way of expressing a deep and heartfelt gratitude for this extraordinary physical and healing art. Pal Dan Gum works. As the saying goes—"Just do it!"

chapter 1

Qi Gong can reveal the mystery of life. It is the best way to further world medical science and bring health, longevity, and wisdom to humankind.
—TZU KUO SHIH

What Is Qi Gong?

For centuries, Oriental medical philosophy has held the belief that a mysterious and invisible energy exists throughout the universe. This vital energy sparks and sustains life and drives the activities of all living things. In the view of the ancient Taoist philosophers, this energy permeates the human organism, making it a vast energetic network. Sages of old knew what modern-day science and theoretical physics have only recently discovered, namely, our bodies and minds are basically fields of energy that vibrate and move at different rates and in different ways. These energy fields are interconnected—they interact with matter, affect one another, and take a particular form that we identify as the human body.

There are certain vital activities that sustain life, such as breathing, eating, drinking, sleeping, thinking, choosing, exercising—any and all of which would cease without a continuous supply of energy. Energy supports and maintains all the vital structures and functions of the body; it is the vital force that nourishes the cells, tissues, and various interacting subsystems of the body (for example, the nervous system, the musculoskeletal system, the circulatory system, and the immune system). This life energy is what the ancients referred to as Qi (pronounced "chee"). In order to define and understand Qi Gong ("chee kung"), we must first define and understand Qi.

qi—the energy of life

The meridian is that which decides over life and death.
—Nei Ching

Ancient Taoist manuscripts put forth the theory of a subtle and formless energy that emanates from the sun, moon, and earth, and that permeates nature. This energy was called "Qi" and is the vital life force that sustains all living things. Qi is what keeps us alive from the moment of our conception to the moment of our death. It is the energy of life, flowing throughout and over the whole body along minute and precise channels called "meridians." These meridians are the rivers and streams of the body—channeling and transporting vital energy to every cell, muscle, organ, and interacting system.

The concept of a life force is central to the belief systems and medical philosophies of many ancient cultures. Qi is called "Chi" in China, "Ki" in Japan, "Prana" in India, "The Great Spirit" in Native America, "Num" in the plateau region of Africa, and "Lapa'au" in the Kahuna shamanic tradition of Hawaii. The ancient Greeks used the word "pneuma" to refer to the vital spirit or invisible energy that holds living things together. Qi is what the French philosopher Henri Bergson called "élan vital," the vital force present in all living things and the source of causation and evolution in nature. Wilhelm Reich, the Austrian psychoanalyst, referred to Qi energy as "orgone," the universal life force emanating from all organic material. He believed that one's physical and emotional well-being depended on the unobstructed flow of biological energy in the body. This aspect of Reich's theory is strikingly similar to Taoist cosmology.

yin and yang—the balance of life

The ten thousand things carry yin and embrace yang.
They achieve harmony by combining these forces.
—LAO TZU
Tao Te Ching (42)

This basic concept of Qi flowing through a meridian system is closely related to the cosmic principles of "yin" and "yang" (yin is pronounced "yeen" and yang is pronounced "yong"). Yin and yang are inseparable tendencies of Qi. They coexist as opposite but complementary forces, like the positive and negative poles of a magnet. According to yin/yang theory, these two forces combine to produce everything in the universe. Not only every thing, but every quality and every situation must have an opposite to balance it out. Thus, everything we see and experience is both a union of opposites and a balancing act of nature—heaven balances earth, day balances night, hot balances cold. Yin is the soft, feminine, calm, and dark cosmic principle—a quality of night, moon, and water. Yang is the hard, masculine, energetic, and light cosmic principle—a quality of day, sun and fire.

The yin/yang symbol represents the Taoist theory of the universe set forth in the *I Ching* (*Book of Changes*, from approximately 1000 years BC). Yin and yang express that life is a process and we are but one part of that process. There is a continuous give and take between what is yin and what is yang, and the interplay between these two forces is the dance of life. The yin/yang symbol flows accordingly—the black (yin) portion flows into the white, and the white (yang) portion flows into the black. That each portion flows into the other represents the fact that the universe is constantly in flux and that change is inevitable. That each portion restricts the other reminds us that yin and yang are inseparable forces; neither exists independently of the other (there is no earth without the heavens, night without day, male without female).

The yin/yang symbol represents the principles and dynamics governing the universe. That it is a circle speaks to the balance and wholeness of nature

The Yin/Yang Symbol

as well as the eternal oneness of the universe. The symbol is thus a way of clarifying the relationship between the parts of a whole, whether the whole is the entire earth's ecosystem or an individual human body. Following the circle around, and around again, the yin/yang symbol becomes a spiral of change: Yin turns into yang which turns into yin which turns into yang, and so on, endlessly. The white dot on the black background and the black dot on the white background remind us that even when one force is dominant, all things contain the other force as well. The ideal in the universe and in life is to be both yin and yang, to strike the right balance and be in harmony. For example, in American culture (generally speaking) men tend to be too masculine and women tend to be too feminine; both need to balance themselves by developing their opposite sides.

Yin/yang theory is the fundamental principle of Oriental medical philosophy. It applies to all natural methods of healing, such as Qi Gong, acupuncture, acupressure, massage, and herbology. *When yin and yang are balanced, the Qi flows freely and we enjoy good health. When yin and yang are out of balance, Qi is blocked and illness results.* Free-flowing Qi means that healing energy can get to the places in the body that most need it. If the flow of Qi along a particular meridian is deficient (too yin) or excessive (too yang), the organ system nourished by that meridian will lose its vitality. When the delicate balance between yin and yang is restored, vitality will return. If energy ceases to flow altogether, then death will result. By living in balance and harmony with ourselves and our universe, we can attain vibrant health and long life.

the law of the five elements

You already have the precious mixture that will make you well. Use it.
—RUMI

Yin and yang combine to produce everything and the interactions between the two forces follow a natural cycle. This cycle operates in accord with the physical elements found in nature—water, wood, fire, earth, and metal—the Five Elements. Taken literally, these elements are the basic components or building blocks of the universe—the "stuff" that makes up the material world. The Five Elements are inherent in all living matter, which organizes into organic wholes. Taken symbolically, each of the Five Elements represents a force, or a movement of energy:

Creation and Destruction of the Five Elements

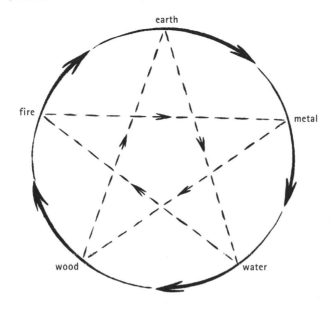

- Water represents energy descending
- Wood represents energy expanding
- Fire represents energy ascending
- Earth represents energy connecting
- Metal represents energy solidifying

According to Taoist cosmology, everything that happens in the universe is regulated by these different movements of energy; this is called "The Law of The Five Elements." These five movements of energy form an elaborate system of mutual interaction and influence, and any reference to one movement of energy is a reference to all because they are functionally interdependent. This means that the energies in the universe and in our bodies are always coming into mutual relationship and affecting one another, simultaneously rising up, sinking down, expanding, solidifying, and connecting.

The Law of The Five Elements operates as a Law of Creation and a Law of Destruction (see diagram). To ensure that one movement of energy does not become too weak or passive (yin), or too strong or dominant (yang), each element has both a creative and a destructive cycle. In the creative cycle (outside arrows), each element has the essential quality of creativity as it interacts with another element. This means that each element uses its energy to "create" another element which, in turn, creates another. Thus, water gives birth to wood; wood makes fire; fire produces earth; earth generates metal; and metal nourishes water. In the destructive cycle (inside arrows of diagram), each element uses its energy in order to control or "destroy" another element. Water extinguishes fire; fire melts metal; metal cuts wood; wood restrains earth; and earth consumes water.

The Taoists apply these cycles of creation and destruction to understand and explain everything that happens in the universe, from the movement of the stars to the flow of Qi in the human body. As an example, consider each element and how it corresponds to the cycles of the seasons and an associated color. Water dominates in winter and corresponds with the color blue; wood dominates in spring and corresponds with green; fire dominates in summer and corresponds with red; earth dominates in late summer and corresponds with yellow; and metal dominates in autumn and corresponds with white or gold. This demonstrates how the progression of the seasons naturally follows the five movements of energy, for example, the (blue) water of winter descends into the ground to create the expanding (green) wood of spring.

The Five Elements regulating the universe likewise regulate the body and the mind. This means the different movements of energy not only influence natural events, but they also affect our vital organs, our feelings, and our actions (see the chart below). Every organ system, and the energy channel that nourishes it, is associated with one of the five movements and a corresponding emotion and behavior. A problem with kidney (water) Qi will cause us to experience "sinking" fear, resulting in back pain and groaning behavior. When we have a problem with liver (wood) Qi, anger "expands" until we feel like shouting. Heart (fire) Qi causes joy and laughter to "rise up," but too much fire causes high blood pressure. If we have a problem with spleen (earth) Qi, we will worry and talk too much because we are overly "connected" with our problems. A problem with lung (metal) Qi will cause grief to "solidify" and we will need a good cry.

The Five Elements and their Natural Associations

	water	wood	fire	earth	metal
Energy	Descending	Expanding	Ascending	Connecting	Solidifying
Season	Winter	Spring	Summer	Late Summer	Autumn
Color	Blue	Green	Red	Yellow	White/Gold
Organ	Kidney	Liver	Heart	Spleen	Lung
Emotion	Fear	Anger	Joy	Worry	Grief
Behavior	Groaning	Shouting	Laughter	Talking	Crying

The Taoists consider The Law of The Five Elements to be no less real than the law of gravity. It is not necessary that we thoroughly understand how this law operates, but because health and healing always involve energy transformation, it is important to understand the following basic principles:

- *The human organism functions as a unified whole that is greater than the simple sum of its parts; and*
- *The energies of water, wood, fire, earth, and metal both create and destroy each other to balance the flows of energy throughout the organism.*

This means that if one element (movement of energy) becomes too strong or dominant, an imbalance of yin and yang will result. This, in turn, will obstruct the free flow of Qi to the internal organ corresponding to that element and symptoms occur. Because the different systems of the body are interdependent, this energetic imbalance will then affect other parts of the whole. For example, an impaired respiratory system will lead to a suppressed immune system.

Health is here again defined as a state of balance, and illness an imbalance, in our body's energy system. To understand The Law of The Five Elements is thus to understand cause and effect as it pertains to indicators of health and symptoms of illness. The law implies we can learn to feel the flow of energy through different parts of our bodies to maintain equilibrium. When we are able to stay in balance we can maintain a relaxed body and a calm mind regardless of circumstances. This is the same holistic approach that first inspired the ancient masters to perform certain body movements in order to build and balance the flow of Qi. We now know what they knew centuries ago—to bring about the state of balance that maintains vibrant health, we need a daily Qi Gong practice.

qi gong: a method of building and balancing energy

If you do external exercises, you must *do internal exercises.*
—TAOIST PROVERB

Qi Gong is sometimes spelled Qigong (all one word), but obviously it is still a combination of "Qi" and "Gong." If Qi is energy, the vital life force, what is Gong? The "Gong" part refers to work or exercise that requires both study and practice; it also means a method of training designed to accomplish a certain skill or objective. It is difficult to give a literal translation of Qi Gong because both parts have so many meanings, but a close approximation is *"a method of building and balancing energy through exercise."* Or, put briefly, Qi Gong means energy work or energy exercise. Defined as such, Qi Gong becomes a general name for many different sets of exercises designed to strengthen and balance the life energy that connects body, mind, and spirit. Common to all such exercises is the role of movement, proper breathing, and concentration.

Qi Gong may be practiced in either an active (yang dominant) or passive (yin dominant) way. Active Qi Gong is assertive and dynamic; it involves movement designed to get the Qi flowing freely through the body's energy pathways to promote vibrant health and longevity. Pal Dan Gum is an example of active Qi Gong. Passive Qi Gong is more tranquil and static; it involves no movement (examples are different forms of meditation done while sitting, standing, or lying down). Both active and passive Qi Gong are considered to be methods of "internal" exercise. Whereas "external" exercises such as running, swimming, and karate expend energy, internal exercises build up and balance energy levels. Both active and passive Qi Gong balance yin and yang, but different types of Qi Gong emphasize different goals. Most are designed to promote health and longevity, but in some the emphasis is on developing skill in the martial arts, calming the mind, or striving for spiritual enlightenment.

history of qi gong

Qi Gong has a long and fascinating history, although its exact origins are lost in the mists of time. It is generally believed to be five thousand years old, but some historians suggest it may have originated during the Stone Age, ten thousand years ago! The written history of Qi Gong began almost three thousand years ago when the Chinese people were introduced to the principles of yin and yang in the *I Ching* (*Book of Changes*). During that period of time, dance-like movements and animal-like postures were used to improve circulation and promote overall health.

Around the time of Christ, the influence of Taoism, Buddhism, and Confucianism grew in the Orient and an era of religious Qi Gong flourished. Each of these religions developed different schools of Qi Gong in accord with their particular philosophies and methods of training. Until fairly recently, the training theories and techniques of religious Qi Gong were kept secret in the temples and monasteries of China. Taoist Qi Gong was probably the original form of training and was designed to improve physical vitality by cultivating the elixirs of life (substances believed to maintain life indefinitely) that reside in the body. It is governed by principles outlined in the *Tao Te Ching* (the esoteric Chinese philosophy written by Lao Tzu in the sixth century BC) and emphasized gentle movement, relaxation, and a practical spirituality. Buddhism from India led to a form of Qi Gong that encouraged more active and dynamic movements, mental concentration, and spiritual enlightenment. The Confucians practiced Qi Gong to improve character and produce a "superior person," as indicated by an ethical and intellectual approach to life. There may be thousands of ways to practice Qi Gong, but most trace their historical roots back to the Taoist and Buddhist schools.

The religious Qi Gong era lasted roughly from the time of the Han Dynasty (approximately 206–220 BC) until the Liang Dynasty (approximately 502–557 AD). It gradually gave way to a style that could be used by martial artists who wished to build muscle power to become better fighters. The martial art era of Qi Gong was heavily influenced by the theories and techniques of the Taoist and Buddhist schools; Qi Gong exercises were performed with single-pointed concentration to develop exceptional physical ability and fighting skill. Shaolin Kung Fu, popularized in the 1970s television series "Kung Fu," is perhaps the oldest and best known form of Martial Art Qi Gong. Interestingly, at the Shaolin Temple in Henan, China, there are statues of monks performing Qi Gong movements that are strikingly similar to the exercises taught in this book. This serves as a reminder that, although there are many forms and different schools of Qi Gong, they all evolved from the Taoist and Buddhist schools.

The next era of Qi Gong practice emphasized the medical benefits of the physical arts. In the course of teaching and observing, Taoist healers discovered that certain sets of exercises not only promoted health, but healed illness (Sung, Gin, and Yuan Dynasties; 960 AD to 1368 AD). From their observations came medical Qi Gong, based primarily on the philosophy of Taoism and medical knowledge of Qi circulation. During this period many improvements were made in acupuncture theory and technique. Similar advances were made in understanding the human body and many new methods of Qi Gong were founded, emphasizing active meditation-in-motion rather than passive sitting meditation. Medical Qi Gong thus uses energy exercises to strengthen and balance Qi, improve respiration and circulation, and stimulate the immune system. This trend continued until the end of the Ching Dynasty (1911 AD) when Qi Gong became the object of rigorous scientific study. At present, Qi Gong training theory focuses on various methods of training the body, the mind, the breath, and the Qi to maintain vibrant health and heal illness.

the three treasures of qi gong

In order to accomplish the goal of oneness with the universe, we must actively work on all three of these aspects or spheres by participating in the deep eternal glow of universal life.

—Maoshing Ni

Qi Gong can also be defined as the art of developing what the ancients called the "three treasures of life"—Jing (essence), Qi (energy), and Shen (spirit). This is a more esoteric definition of Qi Gong, little understood outside of Taoist temples and monasteries. It refers to the view that Qi Gong, practiced properly, is a spiritual practice as well as a method of building and balancing energy. Jing, Qi, and Shen are considered by Taoists to be the roots of our lives and therefore the most important aspects of being human. Our roots require strengthening and protection if we are ever to achieve vibrant health and enlightenment. In order to understand the spiritual aspect of Qi Gong, a simple understanding of the three treasures and the relationship between them is necessary.

- *Jing* (essence): *Jing is the substantive essence or genetic potential of the physical body.* Congenital (sometimes called original) Jing is inherited from one's parents and determines one's basic strength. It is the most important essence because it corresponds to sexual energy, the elemental root of life. Acquired Jing comes from the nutrients and minerals in the food we eat and from the oxygen in the air we breathe. Serious Qi Gong practitioners are mindful of what they eat and how their food is prepared because nutrient intake affects acquired Jing. Similarly, they preserve congenital Jing by refraining from sexual misconduct and avoiding excessive sexual activity. Qi Gong practice seeks to conserve Jing and then convert it into Qi.

- *Qi* (energy): *Qi is the vital force that permeates nature and is the mobilizing function of all life.* Life is considered a coming together of Qi and health is a manifestation of Qi flowing freely through the energy channels of the body. Illness is a manifestation of Qi flow that has become weak, blocked, or out of balance. Death results from the total dispersion of Qi from the body. Two sources supply the human body with its reservoir of Qi: congenital (sometimes called original) Qi is inherited from our parents and comes with our chromosomes. It includes both strong and weak elements and thus affects our constitution. This is why Qi Gong practice can help to strengthen congenital weaknesses such as postural misalignment or asthma.

Acquired Qi, the second source of Qi in the body, comes from the food we eat, the water we drink, and the air we breathe. Eating nutritious food and breathing properly allows us to strengthen the Qi in our bodies by building our reservoir of acquired Qi. Because we have immediate control over how we eat and breathe, and because these activities have an immediate effect on our bodies, acquired Qi is typically the first to benefit from Qi Gong practice. Whereas we cannot increase the amount of Jing we have in our bodies (though we can conserve what we already have), we can increase the amount of Qi we have through Qi Gong practice. A good supply of Qi nourishes the brain and sharpens the mind so it can be converted into Shen.

• *Shen* (spirit): *Shen is the spiritual power or the divine in-dwelling that guides us.* It exists as an energetic phenomenon and is said to reside just behind the place on the forehead commonly known as the third eye. Shen is the force that keeps our fields of energy vibrating and our vital activities operating. Congenital Shen is sparked by the union of male and female essence as sperm meets egg—a gift from our parents. Acquired Shen is generated after birth as we interact with the environment and can be thought of as mental activity. Because our minds are untrained, we are constantly subjected to uninvited and disturbing mental activity. This comes to us both consciously and unconsciously through thoughts, memories, desires, plans, expectations, disappointments, judgments, resentments, and regrets. We can learn to use Acquired Shen wisely by quieting the mind and learning to detach. Detachment means I experience my thoughts and emotions, but I am *not* my thoughts and emotions—I am essence, energy, and spirit! By raising up the Shen we learn to direct and invest our energy with loving-kindness in order to maintain health and promote longevity.

Jing, Qi, and Shen coexist in our being. Where there is essence, there must be energy and spirit; where there is energy, there must be essence and spirit; where there is spirit, there must be essence and energy. According to Taoist philosophy, these three treasures of life are the roots of our lives and the foundation for making Qi Gong a spiritual (as well as physical) art. *Qi Gong training is a way to conserve our essence, balance our energy, and raise up our spirit.* These are both the goals and benefits of Qi Gong and why the spiritual journey begins with everyday practice. These benefits can be achieved by beginning and intermediate Qi Gong practitioners who read and use this book.

Advanced practitioners (those who make Qi Gong a lifetime practice) are always mindful of working on and strengthening their roots. Through practice they learn the art of converting Jing (essence) into Qi (energy) to nourish the brain and raise up the Shen (spirit). This process of conversion is sometimes referred to as "three flowers (treasures) meeting at the top of the head." Only when the three flowers are gathered at the top can the practitioner reach the ultimate goal of enlightenment. The Taoists believe that all living things contain the three treasures, but only human beings are capable of attaining the Supreme Consciousness of the Universe. This is more commonly known as "becoming one with the Tao"—the ultimate state in which one has achieved harmony, detachment, enlightenment, and joy.

summary or oriental medical philosophy

The occurrence of disease is due to insufficiently balanced qi.
—Nei Ching

To summarize Oriental medical philosophy, Qi is both the energy of nature and the vital life force that flows throughout the human body. When the complementary but opposite forces of yin and yang are in balance, the Qi flows freely through the body's energy pathways and we enjoy vibrant health. Illness results when Qi becomes blocked or out of balance and death results when the flow of Qi stops altogether. Qi Gong is an ancient practice. It means "energy work," or "energy exercise," and may be practiced in either an active (more yang) or passive (more yin) way. Active Qi Gong refers to many different sets of exercises that emphasize the role of movement, breathing, and concentration. Passive Qi Gong does not involve movement and refers to the many meditative practices that calm and empty the mind. As a physical art, Qi Gong is the method of building and balancing the body's energy to promote health and heal illness. As a spiritual practice, it is a way of developing one's essence, energy, and spirit to live in harmony with ourselves and the world.

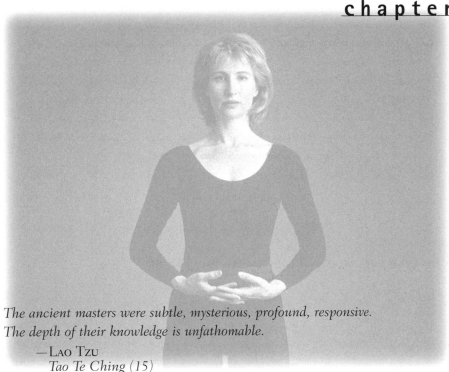

chapter 2

The ancient masters were subtle, mysterious, profound, responsive.
The depth of their knowledge is unfathomable.

—LAO TZU
    Tao Te Ching (15)

What Is Pal Dan Gum?

Pal Dan Gum, or Eight Silken Movements, is an ancient form of Qi Gong consisting of a sequence of eight gentle exercises. It is an effective and proven method of training the body, the breath, the mind, and the Qi to improve health and longevity. It is easy to learn, fun to do, and takes only six minutes from start to finish. A full definition of Pal Dan Gum must also take into account the following:

1. *It is an active form of Qi Gong* practice in that it involves a sequence of dynamic movements performed while standing.
2. *It is a set of "internal" exercises* designed to improve the health of mind and body. Although the movements look like ordinary exercise that expends energy, they are not, because their intent is to use external movement to energize the body and calm the mind.
3. *It is a type of medical Qi Gong* that adjusts the acupuncture points and energy channels of the body to build and balance Qi, thus promoting health and healing illness.

4. *It is considered a complete and holistic system of Qi Gong training* in that it activates all twenty of the body's energy channels to thoroughly balance the flow of Qi (other forms of Qi Gong only activate specific channels).

5. *Its origin is the Taoist school of Qi Gong* because it is based on the fundamental principles of Taoism, namely, the concept of Qi as the life force connecting body, mind, and spirit as one inseparable whole, yin/yang theory, and a practical spirituality, emphasizing harmony with nature.

6. *Pal Dan Gum is a meditation-in-motion* and, as such, a spiritual discipline that cultivates the three treasures (essence, energy, and spirit) to move the practitioner along the path toward enlightenment.

the origins of pal dan gum

As with most ancient forms of Qi Gong, the exact origins of Pal Dan Gum are unknown. However, the eight Pal Dan Gum movements are clearly derived from a set of sixty-four movements called *Ba Gong Dao-In*, which roughly translated means "Energy Conducting Exercises from the Immortal School." According to living Taoist master Hua-Ching Ni, Ba Gong Dao-In is at least six thousand years old! Its sixty-four movements were first patterned after movements occurring spontaneously in nature. Hence, these movements were given names like "The Weeping Willow Shivers in the Early Morning Breeze," and "The Great Bird Spreads Its Wings." This emulation of movements seen in nature reflects the Taoist goal of restoring the body to its intrinsic state of balance and harmony.

An unknown Taoist is credited with taking the eight most essential and beneficial of the sixty-four movements that made up Ba Gong Dao-In and creating an abbreviated version. This set was called *Ba Duan Jin*, which means "Brocade Exercises in Eight Forms in Standing Position," or simply "The Eight Pieces of Silk Brocade." Brocade is a colorful silk fabric that is interwoven with an intricate raised design (as depicted on the front cover of this book). It has always been highly treasured in the Orient and was here used as a metaphor for vibrant health—which was also treasured as an essential component of spiritual enlightenment.

According to Chinese folklore, Chong Li-quan, a general in the Chinese army during the Han Dynasty (206 BC–220 AD), was one of the first to learn and master Ba Duan Jin. As the story goes, Chong, who was intent on expanding the national territory of China, suffered a crushing defeat at the hands of the rival Tibetans. Rather than return to Beijing and face the wrath of the Emperor, Chong went into hiding in the mountains of Southern China. There he became the student of an enlightened Taoist who taught him Qi Gong methods to cultivate the elixirs of life (substances that bestow immortality) that reside in the body. One of these methods was Ba Duan Jin. After learning to live in perfect harmony with nature, Chong became one of the Eight Immortals (or Eight Old Ones) of traditional Chinese mythology. Before his death, he diagrammed the sequence of eight exercises on the walls of a cave that was discovered several centuries later by another Chinese general, Lu Dong-bin. General Lu mastered the exercises, also became one of the Eight Immortals, and was the first to inscribe Ba Duan Jin on stone.

Ba Duan Jin first appears in writing in an eighth century Taoist text, *Ten Treatises on Restoring Original Vitality*. It is also explained in an ancient Chinese text called the *Dao Shu*, compiled during the Southern Song Dynasty (1127–1279 AD). This version is derived from still another Chinese military hero, Marshal Yeuh Fei (1103–1142 AD). He recorded each of the movements in the form of a poem that explained its execution and purpose, and taught them to his soldiers to improve their health, stamina, and martial art skills. Yeuh Fei and his army became legendary for expelling barbarians from the north (the Gin race) who had successfully invaded China. Yeuh Fei and his men were never defeated in battle, a fact attributed to his military genius and the rigorous Qi Gong training he expected of his men. Tragically, his reward for serving his country so well was to be murdered by the prime minister of the Emperor's corrupt court.

Pal Dan Gum, or The Eight Silken Movements, is the Korean version of Ba Duan Jin. As with most forms of Qi Gong, Pal Dan Gum has undergone numerous modifications and refinements as the "original" was passed from stone to paper, master to student, parent to child, generation to generation. Over the centuries, Pal Dan Gum has evolved into a uniquely Korean form of Qi Gong and it differs from the Chinese form, Ba Duan Jin, in several ways. The key differences are that the eight movements of Pal Dan Gum are performed with fewer repetitions, with a specific number of repetitions, in a different sequence, and in a more dynamic way, with more force or vigor. Pal Dan Gum and Ba Duan Jin now appear to be different versions of the same set of movements. This is of no real consequence to the practitioner, because the fundamental principles and the benefits are pretty much the same.

How and when Pal Dan Gum became a form of Korean Qi Gong is unknown, although the geography and history of Korea may offer a clue. Korea is a peninsula (about the size of the state of Minnesota) extending out from the mainland of China between the Yellow Sea and Sea of Japan. Korea is only

400 miles from Beijing, the ancient capital of China. The present-day Korean peninsula is the site of an ancient civilization (known as the Hermit Kingdom) that dates back to the twelfth century BC. Its proximity to Beijing is significant because Korea was part of the Chinese empire until it became united as a separate kingdom in the seventh century AD. Since Beijing was both a commercial and cultural center and since what is now Korea was relatively close to Beijing, the early inhabitants of Korea would have been familiar with the Taoist healing arts and the philosophy upon which they were based. Thus, Qi Gong practitioners in Korea almost certainly would have been exposed to both the popular Ba Gong Dao-In and Ba Duan Jin. Over time, they would modify and refine the eight movements until making Pal Dan Gum their own.

comparison to t'ai chi chuan

Pal Dan Gum is the most popular form of Qi Gong in Korea, whereas T'ai Chi Chuan (T'ai Chi) is most popular in China. T'ai Chi is an ancient Chinese energy exercise that requires slow, deliberate, and continuous shadow-boxing movements and looks like a graceful dance routine. T'ai Chi was originally a form of martial art Qi Gong, but as now practiced, there is little emphasis on fighting. Rather, it emphasizes health and vitality by developing internal stillness. This has brought T'ai Chi practice closer to Pal Dan Gum, and they can be thought of as different branches on the same tree, or Qi Gong first cousins. Both are gentle, non-impact forms of exercise performed while standing (many forms of Qi Gong are done in a sitting position). Both require the practitioner to execute a specific sequence of deliberate, slow-motion body movements. Both are earthy and grounded meditations-in-motion that teach a way to approach life with balance and harmony. Each form encourages attention to the breath, present-centeredness, and single-pointed concentration. Fundamental to both is the Taoist principle that the Qi flows freely when the opposite yet complementary forces of yin and yang are in balance. Both teach that by building and balancing Qi throughout the body we maintain vibrant health.

Despite the similarities between Pal Dan Gum and T'ai Chi, there are also significant differences. Of course, the actual body movements are different, but more important, Pal Dan Gum is a sequence of eight separate, individual body movements. It is like pulling silk from a cocoon—one pulls then pauses, pulls then pauses. By comparison, T'ai Chi cannot be separated into individual movements because it is a series of movements that connect from beginning to end. T'ai Chi is thus like the flow of water, moving smoothly with unbroken continuity. Another difference is that T'ai Chi requires a gentle slowness, with fluid and graceful body movements. Pal Dan Gum movements also flow smoothly from one to the next, but in between there is an emphasis on holding stretches in order to increase flexibility, strength, and power. This makes Pal Dan Gum more like a set of exercises or a form of calisthenics; it requires more exertion and is therefore the more dynamic type of training. The point is not that one is better than the other, but that despite many similarities, Pal Dan Gum and T'ai Chi are different schools or branches of Qi Gong.

For breath is life, and if you breathe well you will live long on earth.
—SANSKRIT PROVERB

Training Your Breath

The breath is not just fundamental to life, or an expression of life, it is life itself. This is why Qi is sometimes translated as "vital breath." The components of the breath—inhalation and exhalation, expansion and contraction, yin and yang—sustain the natural pulsation that keeps us alive. How we inhale and exhale, and how effectively we use the air we exchange, plays an essential role in all our physical activities, not to mention how we think, feel, and relate to others. This is apparent in the ways we use everyday language to express how certain breath patterns affect our bodies and minds. "Breathing easy" or "breathing a sigh of relief" means we feel relaxation after a period of tension. We say we are "out of breath" or "gasping for air" to communicate breathing with difficulty after exerting ourselves. If I say the boss is "full of hot air" or "breathing down my neck," everyone knows what I mean. These expressions would seem to imply we recognize the importance of the breath, yet our own breathing pattern is usually so involuntary and unconscious that we take it for granted.

An experience in 1982 awakened me from this mindless attitude of unconscious breathing. My beloved little Tonkinese cat gave birth to a litter of four kittens. Instinctively, she ruptured each fluid-filled sac and licked each kitten until it would begin to squirm and breathe. All were strong and healthy except one that appeared to be stillborn. However, close examination revealed an ever-so-faint breath. Acting as midwife, I cradled the kitten in my palm and swung it back and forth several times to clear its air passages, then began gentle squeezing to stimulate its breathing reflex. Then, for some time, my wife and my mother took turns holding it over a heating vent and rubbing it briskly with a rough towel until its breathing became stronger. In an hour it was breathing on its own, and several days later we couldn't distinguish it from its litter mates. This kitten would have died if we had allowed nature to take its course. Our efforts to stimulate its breathing had sparked its fragile life and its will to survive took over from there. Never have I been more acutely aware that breath is life and, ever since, I have worked at becoming more conscious of my own breathing patterns.

How we breathe during any waking moment is under both voluntary and involuntary control, yet we seldom pay attention to our breath pattern unless we are breathing with difficulty. There is a Zen story about a student who complained to the master that paying attention to the breath was boring. The Zen master proceeded to submerge the student's head in water and held him under while the student struggled to come up for air. After holding him under for some time, he let the gasping student up and asked him if he found breathing boring or interesting while he was under water. The student got the point and the breath became a great teacher for him.

Attention on the breath is both interesting and useful. It reminds us that we are here now, and that we can be more aware of whatever else is happening in the moment. When we are more conscious of how we breathe, we shift attention to and feel more at home in our bodies. This makes it more likely we will breathe properly and support the basic physiological processes of our bodies and minds. Proper breathing will not only regulate our heartbeat, but improve blood circulation to supply our cells, tissues, and organs with all the oxygen they need. Unfortunately, most people maintain an improper breathing pattern characterized by inhaling into the upper chest rather than the abdomen. Since we inhale and exhale more than 1,000 timer per hour and take more than 25,000 breaths per day, breathing properly and regulating our breathing pattern may be the single most important thing we can do to improve our health.

regulating the breath

Breathing control gives man strength, vitality, inspiration, and magic powers.
—CHUANG TZU

The concept of regulating the breath is central to all Qi Gong practices, including Pal Dan Gum. To regulate means to direct according to a principle in order to bring about proper functioning. To regulate the breath means retraining your breathing pattern until it is proper. Breathing pattern refers primarily to how rapidly we inhale and exhale and whether the predominant movements during inhalation and exhalation occur in our chest or abdomen. It also refers to how the breath feels to the breather—shallow or deep, incomplete or complete, noisy or quiet, labored or easy. The ancient masters summarized the keys to breath regulation in three words. They are:

1. *Slender: Whenever possible, breathe in and out through your nasal passageways to make the breath a slender, thread-like stream.* Your mouth should be gently closed with a soft jaw, tongue gently touching the roof of your mouth. This approach makes for a longer and more uniform breath. It also filters the air, regulates air temperature, and relaxes your body and mind. If you need to breathe through your mouth, avoid gulping air by gently pursing your lips so the inflow of air will be a slender stream.

2. *Silent: Your breathing should be silent, soft, and easy.* This automatically slows your breathing rate and cultivates a meditative state of stillness and tranquillity.

3. *Deep: Take long, slow, deep breaths way down into your abdomen.* This does not mean inhaling to the bursting point or holding your breath! It means gently concentrating on slowing and deepening your inhalation to become an abdominal breather.

Once you understand these keys, and learn to take slender, silent, and deep breaths, you will be using a proper breathing pattern. Regulating the breath will allow you to better absorb oxygen and Qi from the air to improve health and vitality.

Unfortunately, people today are chronically stressed and distressed and we typically breathe in a way that violates all three keys to regulation. Most commonly, we take shallow and rapid breaths into the upper chest. This causes our upper chest to expand as we inhale, but not our abdomen, so we only fill the upper portion of our lungs. This means we take in and exchange less volume of air and have less oxygen available for the production of energy. Oxygen fuels the energy-making processes in the trillions of cells that make up our bodies. Just as a candle burns brighter in a room with plentiful oxygen, the human body needs a good supply of oxygen to keep its metabolic fires burning. This need is demonstrated by the fact that we can survive for days without food and water, but brain cells cannot survive more than a few minutes without oxygen and the body will expire soon thereafter. Thus, proper breathing is not only crucial to good health, but to life itself.

Because our lungs are called upon to exchange over 10,000 gallons of air every day of our lives, efficient respiration becomes an important consideration for health. If we are breathing improperly, and most of us are, we will experience significant oxygen deprivation and a consequent lack of support for our basic physiological processes. For example, there are trillions of connecting points between nerve cells in the brain. An oxygen fueled, spark-like reaction occurs at each of these connections, enabling us to think, feel, act, and function. Thus, any tendency toward oxygen deprivation results in chronic physical and mental fatigue, anxiety and muscular tension, a suppressed immune system, and susceptibility to all kinds of illness. Furthermore, upper chest breathing automatically sends stress signals to our brain and triggers the production of "fight or flight" hormones that lead to unwanted and unhealthy changes. They are, to name a few, increased heart rate, elevated blood pressure, diffuse physiological arousal, decreased cell production and repair, and decreased sexual processes. Conversely, when we breathe more slowly and deep down into the abdomen, our brain and nervous system receive "okay" signals telling us it is safe to relax.

abdominal (dan tien) breathing

The men of old breathed clear down to their heels.
—CHUANG TZU

If the most common pattern is shallow and rapid upper chest breathing, what would constitute proper breathing? *Proper breathing is the activity of taking in and exchanging a maximum of air with a minimum of effort.* To do this we must understand the art and science of breath control; this means retraining and regulating our pattern by taking slender, silent, and deep breaths. Making this change is easier when we understand something of the anatomy and physiology of the respiratory process. The chest and abdomen are separated by a dome-shaped and muscular partition called the diaphragm. In abdominal breathing, the abdomen expands outward and the diaphragm descends during inhalation. Then, during exhalation, the pattern is reversed—the abdomen contracts inward and the diaphragm ascends (see photos on page 29). These actions allow the sack-like lungs to function like bellows, sucking in fresh air and oxygen and expelling used air and carbon dioxide. Breathing mindfully into the abdomen improves respiratory efficiency and brings about a maximal exchange of air.

From a physical standpoint, abdominal breathing is easy because it is actually re-learning a natural and instinctual pattern that is hard-wired into the human organism (watch how an infant breathes abdominally). However, many people find it difficult to let go of the idea that it is unattractive for the abdomen to expand out during inhalation. The cultural ideal of "fronting" with a flat stomach requires that we expend a great deal of effort and energy to oppose our natural tendency to relax the abdomen as we breathe. Cultural pressures to achieve an ideal body-image and appear thin cause men and women alike to feel self-conscious about letting their bellies out during the in-breath, especially if they are already overweight. This attitude must shift if we are to breathe as nature intends and enjoy the many health benefits of proper breathing. I tell my Qi Gong students they will not be able to concentrate on taking a slender, silent, and deep breath—and worry about how it looks at the same time.

Abdominal breathing is proper breathing and is essential for vibrant health. It is done slowly; the breath is drawn deep down into the abdomen, and we make a complete exhalation before the next inhalation. We breathe slowly by "slowing down time" and taking eight or fewer breaths per minute (about half our usual rate). With practice, most people become able to take only three or four breaths per minute without any sensations of discomfort or air hunger. As we draw in a deep breath, our diaphragm descends so that the inhaled air fills both the upper *and lower* portion of our lungs. Our exhale is mainly the passive and effortless process of letting go of used air. A slow and deep inhalation with a slow and complete exhalation yields maximum efficiency from the air we exchange, thus supporting basic physiological processes for optimal heart rate and blood circulation. This breathing pattern yields predictable physical and psychological benefits and has been successfully used in treating disorders ranging from coronary heart disease to panic attacks.

Abdominal breathing is but one of many breathing techniques developed by Qi Gong masters to regulate the breath. It promotes a pattern whereby the inhalation is slowly drawn into the area just below the navel; this area is called the "Dan Tien" in Chinese ("Dan Jun" in Korean, "hara" in Japanese). Dan Tien means "Field of Elixir" and refers to the region believed by Taoist alchemists to contain substances that bestow immortality. That region is approximately an inch or two below the navel and approximately two to four inches deep, depending on body type. The Dan Tien is the place in our bodies where the passive force of yin and the active force of yang are perfectly balanced. This makes the Dan Tien the most important energy center in the human body. It has also been called the "Sea of Qi," "Center of Vital Energy," and the "Golden Stove That Burns Out Disease"—descriptions that convey yin/yang thinking and its importance in maintaining health and healing illness.

abdominal breathing

To feel the sensations of abdominal breathing, lie on your back with your knees bent and your feet flat on the floor. Place a book on your abdomen directly over your navel but low enough so that it is not resting on your lower rib cage. Take a slow and deep inhalation and notice how the book rises as your abdomen expands (see the following photos).

Now make a slow and thorough exhalation and notice how the book moves downward as your abdomen contracts.

Your chest should barely move during inhalation and exhalation. Notice the internal sensations of your diaphragm descending during inhalation and ascending during exhalation. You can train yourself to be an abdominal breather by practicing this simple exercise.

Caution: While learning abdominal breathing, a few people experience light-headedness, headache, or even strong emotions. Should you experience these or similar symptoms, or if you have a history of respiratory difficulties, consult an appropriate health care professional before continuing.

pausal abdominal breathing

Breathe the old out and the new in.
—TAOIST PRACTICE OF *Tu Na*

While performing Pal Dan Gum we are encouraged to breathe into the Dan Tien, pausing briefly between inhalation and exhalation—a method called pausal abdominal breathing. Pausal abdominal breathing is slow, deep, abdominal breathing that incorporates a slight pause between each inhalation and exhalation, and between each exhalation and inhalation. This ensures that our

Inhalation

Exhalation

breathing is consistently smooth and continuous, thus promoting relaxation and emotional control. The pausal breathing pattern is therefore:

Inhale…Pause…Exhale…Pause…Inhale…Pause…Exhale…
and so on, with a slight pause at the end of each
inhalation and exhalation.

This pattern of breathing differs from normal abdominal breathing in that it requires a bit of concentration to slow down and deepen the breath, then pause at the end of inhaling just before you exhale. These pauses typically occur in a natural and spontaneous way as we concentrate on making a slow and deep inhalation into the Dan Tien, then making a long and slow exhalation. Pausing is not the same as holding our breath (which is discouraged in Qi Gong), but a hesitation or moment of rest in the breath pattern. The image of a pendulum comes to mind. As it swings freely back and forth under the influence of gravity, it makes a momentary pause every time it changes direction. The same image applies to pausal abdominal breathing. Air moves freely in and out of our lungs under the influence of breathing, and we make an ever-so-slight pause in changing from inhalation to exhalation, and exhalation to inhalation. This is considered a proper breathing pattern because it meets the requirements of taking in a maximum amount of oxygen with a minimal amount of effort.

Pausal abdominal breathing is said to massage the internal organs, increase positive Qi in the body, and release negative Qi from the body. One reason for keeping the mouth closed while breathing is that it allows positive Qi to flow down to the Dan Tien for storage and negative Qi to discharge into the earth through our legs and feet. Remember, our bodies must continually breathe in oxygen and breathe out carbon dioxide to build up and store the Qi that sustains our life. As we breathe all the way down to the Dan Tien, the abdomen expands outward, causing fresh air (oxygen) to be drawn into the upper *and lower* portions of our lungs. As we exhale, the abdomen contracts and this forces used air (carbon dioxide) out of our lungs. The repetitive movements of expansion and contraction stimulate the Dan Tien to enhance the functions of all our internal organs, one of the primary benefits of pausal abdominal breathing.

To feel the internal movements and sensations of a pausal abdominal breath pattern, we will borrow an imagery exercise used by professional singers and others who train the human voice to convert breath into energy. Begin by imagining that a balloon occupies the area of your lower abdominal cavity (the Dan Tien). Inhale slowly and softly and feel the balloon inflate and expand deep in your belly (your lower back will also expand with each inhalation). Notice that your chest slightly expands as you inflate the balloon. If you attempt to breathe only into your abdomen by keeping your chest rigid, you will exchange less air and send a stress signal to your brain. After inhaling, pause for a moment when the balloon feels comfortably full, then let go and slowly exhale—imagining the balloon deflating until it is empty. Notice that both your abdomen and lower back contract with exhalation. Be sure to make a complete exhalation (without forcing), then pause momentarily and slowly re-inflate the balloon. Repeat this exercise several times. It should be done in a relaxed way using the three keys to regulating the breath. Notice how taking slender, silent, and deep breaths promotes a different pattern from your usual one. Be aware of how good it feels to breathe!

From the beginning of your practice, Pal Dan Gum teaches you to breathe in a way that promotes vibrant health. *We take one breath per movement—a slow and deep inhalation as we begin a movement, a momentary pause as we hold a stretch, then a slow and complete exhalation as we return to the starting position of that movement.* It requires a bit of concentration to breathe slowly and deeply into the abdomen, and to pause between inhalations and exhalations (and vice versa). After a little practice, you will find yourself paying only passive attention to your breathing pattern, that is, little conscious effort will be needed to breathe slowly and deeply.

Pausal abdominal breathing becomes automatic and habitual—learning takes place as you practice the sequence of movements. We inhale slowly and fill the imaginary balloon deep in the abdomen, pause momentarily while we hold our stretch, exhale slowly and empty the balloon, pause, and do it again. The emphasis on slowing our rate of breathing paces our practice as we do each of the Eight Silken Movements. In Qi Gong, there is no need to "push the river"—it flows by itself.

benefits of pausal abdominal breathing

> *Only those who know* how to breathe *will survive.*
> — PUNDIT ACHARYA

By training ourselves to use pausal abdominal breathing as we perform the Eight Silken Movements, we return to the natural (Dan Tien) breathing we were born to use. This means we will benefit from a deeper inhalation, a slower breathing rate, and a larger tidal volume of air exchanged in our lungs. With practice, this proper breathing pattern will become habitual and we can expect the following health benefits:

- We boost our energy levels, increase energy storage, and increase our body's ability to utilize oxygen to improve stamina and performance in all our activities—including work-related tasks and sports.
- We decrease our heart rate and lower blood pressure while increasing the flow of blood and oxygen to the heart, brain, and other organs.
- We increase cellular regeneration, a fact of enormous importance when we realize our bodies need to replace approximately 140 billion cells every day of our lives!
- We activate the relaxation response to release muscular tension and achieve peace of mind. This also shuts off the flow of stress hormones, the "fight or flight" compounds that fuel stress-related symptoms such as anxiety disorders, headaches, or hypertension.
- We trigger a flood of pleasure-inducing neurochemicals in the brain to elevate our mood and combat physical pain.
- We bring our bodies and minds into harmony to enhance spiritual growth—a benefit known and taught by yogis, monks, and meditation teachers for centuries.
- Finally, and perhaps most importantly, proper breathing increases the production of various immune system cells, promoting healing and strengthening our resistance to disease.

These benefits are supported by modern scientific research that has been replicated many times over, confirming what the ancient masters have known about respiration for thousands of years. These are just the benefits of learning to breathe properly (we have yet to fully discuss the benefits that arise from performing the Qi Gong movements that build and balance the Qi in your body). To maximize these benefits, keep in mind the following principles of breath regulation as you practice Pal Dan Gum:

1. *Slender*—breathe through your nostrils whenever possible.
2. *Silent*—breathe slowly and quietly in a relaxed manner.
3. *Deep*—breathe deeply by letting the breath sink way down into your abdomen.
4. *Empty*—empty the lungs by making a thorough exhalation.
5. *Pause*—pause momentarily between each inhalation and exhalation, and vice versa.

chapter 4

The bodily decrepitude presumed under the myth of aging is not inevitable. It is, by and large, both avoidable and reversible.
—Thomas Hanna

Training Your Body

In Greek mythology, there exists a winged monster known as the Sphinx, with the body of a lion and the head and breasts of a woman. The Sphinx was noted for guarding the gates of Thebes and strangling to death any traveler who could not answer the following riddle: "What is it that has one voice and yet becomes four-footed and two-footed and three-footed?" Oedipus, the son of the King and Queen of Thebes, solved the riddle by answering, "The human being who crawls on all fours as an infant, walks on two legs as an adult, and leans on a cane in old age."

This pessimistic assumption about the process of aging leads us to another and more pertinent question; namely, why must the human organism deteriorate so badly as it ages? The answer to this question is, according to Taoist physicians and healers, that the body need not and should not deteriorate with age. An often quoted Qi Gong proverb tells us the body should remain "supple like an infant," and "flexible like a snake." The key to achieving these lofty goals and preventing the crippling effects of aging is to train the body using the theory and techniques of Qi Gong.

regulating the body

The real regulating happens only when you don't need to consciously regulate.
—Dr. Yang Jwing-Ming

Qi Gong training theory is founded on the concept of regulation, which, as we previously discussed, means to control or adjust according to a principle that ensures proper functioning. Just as there are three keys for proper breathing (keeping the breath slender, silent, and deep), there are also three principles the Qi Gong trainee must learn in order to regulate the body. They are postural alignment, relaxation of the whole body, and developing a strong root (see the photograph of "Standing Like A Tree"). These principles are interrelated: correct posture promotes relaxation, deep relaxation promotes a feeling of rootedness, developing a strong root improves balance and posture—all of which make for free-flowing and healthy Qi. We will examine each principle separately.

Posture

Of the thousands of forms of Qi Gong, there are but four basic postures for regulating the body. These are, in order of most commonly used, standing, sitting, lying, and walking. We have already learned that Pal Dan Gum is an active (movement) form of Qi Gong performed while standing, so this chapter will only consider standing posture (Chapter 9 discusses sitting posture during passive Qi Gong, or sitting meditation).

While performing the Eight Silken Movements it is not necessary or desirable to force your body into any uncomfortable postures or positions. If you find a particular position difficult to get into or hold, simply perform that position as best you can until you become more adept. Qi Gong does not require that you twist your body like a pretzel as do some types of yoga, nor is there any need for intense physical movements as with other forms of exercise. As the saying goes, performing each movement should feel "soft like water" and doing the movements in sequence should feel "like pulling silk from a cocoon."

The first principle of regulating the body is that it must be in the correct posture while performing Qi Gong exercises. Incorrect posture creates bodily tension and a Qi flow that is unbalanced or obstructed. *Correct posture while standing means that the major segments of the body—head, neck, thorax, abdomen, pelvis, and legs—are as close to being vertically aligned as possible.* This correctly aligned posture is the basic starting position in Pal Dan Gum. It

Standing Like a Tree

The "posture of power" in Qi Gong training emphasizes correct postural
alignment, relaxation of the whole body, and developing a strong root.

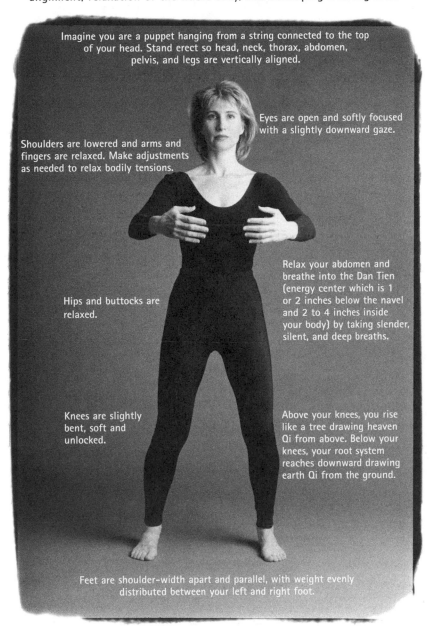

Imagine you are a puppet hanging from a string connected to the top
of your head. Stand erect so head, neck, thorax, abdomen,
pelvis, and legs are vertically aligned.

Eyes are open and softly focused
with a slightly downward gaze.

Shoulders are lowered and arms and
fingers are relaxed. Make adjustments
as needed to relax bodily tensions.

Relax your abdomen and
breathe into the Dan Tien
(energy center which is 1
or 2 inches below the navel
and 2 to 4 inches inside
your body) by taking slender,
silent, and deep breaths.

Hips and buttocks are
relaxed.

Knees are slightly
bent, soft and
unlocked.

Above your knees, you rise
like a tree drawing heaven
Qi from above. Below your
knees, your root system
reaches downward drawing
earth Qi from the ground.

Feet are shoulder-width apart and parallel, with weight evenly
distributed between your left and right foot.

Feel your invisible roots reaching deep down into the earth to give you secure contact
with the ground and a base of support for your whole body.

requires that you stand erect with a straight back so that your *Pai-hui* acupoint (at the top of your head on a line drawn from ear to ear) is vertically in line with your *Hui-yin* acupoint (between the scrotum and the anus in males; between the posterior vulva and the anus in females—the perineum). This is easier than it sounds. Simply align your body in the correct posture by imagining you are a puppet hanging from a string connected to the top of your head. Then remember the following six postural cues:

1. Stand erect, with the top of your head reaching upward, chin drawn slightly in.
2. Keep your head straight, eyes softly focused and gazing slightly downward.
3. Lower your shoulders and allow your arms to hang loosely at your sides, fingers gently spread and relaxed.
4. Relax your abdomen so you can take slender, silent, and deep breaths into your Dan Tien.
5. Relax your hips and buttocks, keeping your knees soft and unlocked.
6. Your feet should be shoulder-width apart and parallel, with your weight evenly distributed between your left and right feet.

According to the Taoists, knowing how to stand with correct posture is an essential aspect of body regulation. This is because it gives you a good start on building up and balancing the natural flow of Qi inside you. It is correct posture that makes it possible to synchronize one of the two main energy circuits within your Qi circulatory system—the "microcosmic orbit." When this orbit is in sync with the rest of the energy circulation system, the Qi flows strongly and smoothly along two primary channels—the Conception (*Ren*) channel and the Governing (*Du*) channel. When the microcosmic orbit is out of sync, the Qi will either "dam up" in the channels, or "leak out," especially at the joints.

The Taoist explanation for how the microcosmic orbit becomes active is as fascinating as it is esoteric. As a beginning Qi Gong practitioner, you will use abdominal breathing and concentration to draw Qi deep into the Dan Tien, the center of vital energy. It is said that one hundred days of practice are required before you will be ready to activate the microcosmic orbit. By then, so much Qi is stored up in the Dan Tien that it overflows the region and moves down the front (*Ren*) channel of your body to the Hui-yin, then up the back (*Du*) channel to the Pai-hui (see illustration of the Microcosmic Orbit). The microcosmic orbit is thus a circle of energy that circulates properly with correct postural alignment. Once activated, its function is to clear or open all the other energy channels in the body to ensure vibrant health.

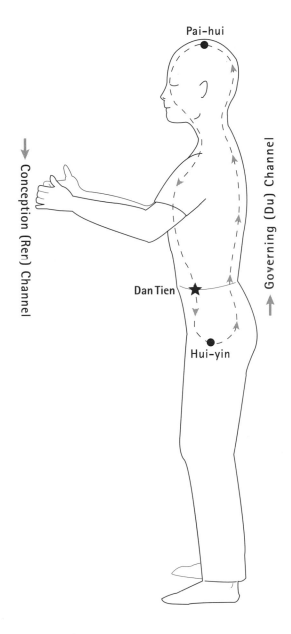

Pai-hui

Conception (Ren) Channel

Governing (Du) Channel

Dan Tien

Hui-yin

The Microcosmic Orbit

Note correct posture, with Pai-hui acupoint vertically in line with Hui-yin acupoint. This allows Qi stored in the Dan Tien to overflow the region and activate a circle of energy flowing down the front channel and up the back channel.

Relaxation

Relaxation is the most important principle of body regulation. As a form of internal exercise, relaxation is the act of relaxing the body to achieve a sense of physical and emotional well-being. Relaxation is also the state of being relaxed, or feeling relief from tension. We have already discussed being relaxed in our posture as one aspect of body regulation; this is accomplished by following the six cues that were given for postural alignment and not straining as we perform our Qi Gong movements. Breathing consciously into your abdomen and concentrating on the internal sensations of body movement support your relaxation. Relax your entire body, but especially your joints—the hinges between bones that allow motion. When your joints are relaxed, open, and unlocked, your Qi can flow freely and you can move gracefully and in balance.

Deeper relaxation involves the musculature and fascia—the connective tissue which binds together our muscles, internal organs, and other soft structures to give the human body its characteristic shape. This deeper relaxation requires some effort, but it is to be a minimum of effort, more of a letting go than of doing something actively. As we let go of tension, deep relaxation really sinks into every muscle, every fiber, and every cell. This has a loosening and softening effect on our body that opens the energy channels for an unobstructed flow of Qi. Advanced practitioners can relax so completely as to intentionally lead the Qi to individual organs and even the bone marrow; this ability requires a trance-like state of mind and a deep stillness of body. Only those who dedicate their lives to Qi Gong practice develop this ability to direct the Qi to a specific target site. However, with practice and sufficient relaxation, we will be able to experience the sensation of Qi moving through our body—most often as warmth, heat, or tingling.

Tension is inevitable because it is a natural response to life stress—the bad events that happen to us, the good events that don't, and our emotional reactions to both. Modern medicine shows that intense or prolonged stress is responsible for a host of physical, psychological, and even social ills. This is because the same fight or flight reflex that gave our caveman ancestors the speed and endurance to escape danger is now activated in situations where it is simply not needed. Thus, stress hormones spill into our bloodstream and stay there much longer than needed to cope with events that could be handled with less bodily alarm. This state of unnecessary arousal and hypervigilance undermines the immune system and leaves us vulnerable to viral infections, psychosomatic illness, and even certain kinds of cancer.

Since we cannot avoid stress, what becomes important is how we meet it when it arises. If we do nothing to manage our stress, judge it as bad, or overreact to it with fear and aversion, our body and mind will suffer. If instead, we notice it mindfully and use it as a cue to relax, we will minimize tension and prevent stress-related illness. *Thus, this aspect of regulation requires that we constantly adjust our body in order to relieve any tension that affects our muscles, joints, nerves, vessels, and internal organs.* Qi Gong is intended to relieve tension and relax the whole body so that Qi can flow freely through the energy channels. Our Qi channels must be open and unobstructed if we are to restore or maintain the delicate balance needed for vibrant health.

Being Rooted

Regulating your body also means developing a strong root so you will feel grounded and stable on your feet. *Rootedness is the sensation of secure contact as our feet touch the ground to provide a base of support for our whole body.* In order to feel rooted we must first be posturally aligned and relaxed, so this aspect of regulation is dependent on those that precede it. If our posture is incorrect, our energy cannot flow freely and connect to the earth, nor will we activate the microcosmic orbit to clear the energy channels. If we are not relaxed we will close off the channels that circulate Qi and preclude good energetic contact with the ground beneath us.

Each of the eight movements that make up Pal Dan Gum requires a strong root in order that we maintain our balance and move correctly. Rootedness gives us a secure two-point base on which to stand and a steady relationship to gravity as we perform Qi Gong movements. To feel rooted in any form of active Qi Gong we are instructed to "stand like a tree" by imagining invisible roots reaching deep down into the earth. Rootedness requires that we allow our body to settle, then center our energy in the Dan Tien and feel our weight sinking through our feet into the ground. This lowers our center of gravity and gives us a better base of support—just as the widest part of the tree is where it contacts the earth. Then, we keep our knees soft and unlocked so energy flows through our legs and feet and into the ground, and vice versa. When we stand like a tree, we draw earth Qi from the ground and heaven Qi from above. Both sources of Qi nourish our roots and expand our energy fields, just as with the trees we imitate. The more effort and intent we put into our Qi Gong practice, the stronger and more developed our root system becomes—a crucial aspect of body regulation.

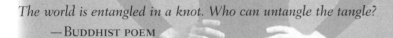

chapter 5

The world is entangled in a knot. Who can untangle the tangle?
    —BUDDHIST POEM

If you want to untie a knot, you must look at the cord carefully and then gently undo the tangle. Yanking on the cord will only make the knot tighter.
    —THOMAS HANNA

Training Your Mind

We are, indeed, "entangled in a knot," and in order to disentangle ourselves we must "look at the cord carefully" by training our minds. As a meditation-in-motion, Pal Dan Gum is a practice that puts us in touch with the only time we have to be alive—the freshness of the present moment. The present is the only time we have to grow, to relax, to heal—to "untangle the tangle." We can heal the past, but we can't heal in the past. We may be healed in the future, but the actual process of healing will take place in a present moment that is either happening right now or has yet to happen. This means we must awaken our minds and pay attention to what is happening and how we are investing our energy in each moment. This is the essence of all forms of meditation.

Kabir said, "You have slept for millions and millions of years. Why not wake up this morning?" This is a good question. People usually stop paying attention for good reasons, or at least reasons that begin with a positive intention. Most often it has to do with avoiding a painful reality in order to protect a vulnerable self against feeling overwhelmed. We try hard to escape painful awareness or conflict, only to find that it is ultimately inescapable. In the end, avoidance only prolongs our suffering—what we really need is to bring a friendly and kind attention to that which causes us to suffer. This strategy asks us to pay "bare attention" to what is happening in the present moment, that is, without adding our reactions to what is happening—a practice called mindfulness. Mindfulness requires that we first awaken from the predicament of not even knowing we are half-asleep—a condition which Buddhists refer to as ignorance. Without awakening, we will be controlled by uninvited and disturbing thoughts, emotions, judgments, expectations, and fantasies. These are the consequences of an untrained and unregulated mind. The choice is ours. We can wake up and pay attention to what happens to us and within us, or remain half-asleep and be tossed about like the proverbial cork on the turbulent sea.

the practice of mindfulness

Pay precise attention, moment by moment, to exactly what you are experiencing, right now, separating out your reactions from the raw sensory events.
—MARK EPSTEIN

In order to train the mind, we must first awaken so that we can be mindful. To accomplish this goal, Qi Gong training theory borrows heavily from the elegant and centuries-old psychology contained in the universal teachings of the Buddha. Not surprisingly, "Buddha" means "one who is awake." There is a story that beautifully illustrates the idea of mindfulness. A visitor asked the Buddha, "What do you and your followers practice that distinguishes your *Sangha* (spiritual community) from others?" The Buddha answered, "We sit, we walk, and we eat." "But sir," the visitor protested, "what's so special about that? Everybody sits, walks, and eats." The Buddha continued, "This is true. But when we sit, we know that we are sitting. When we walk, we know we are walking. And when we eat, we know we are eating."

Mindfulness is the heart of Buddhist meditation, but we don't need to become Buddhists to practice it. When the Buddha says, "when we eat, we know we are eating," he is teaching us that being mindful and aware of our experience, however ordinary that experience is, is the first step in awakening. Mindfulness is a way of waking up to what is really going on within our mind and body. It means giving our wholehearted attention to every aspect of our experience whether it is extraordinary or ordinary, pleasurable or painful, positive or negative. Eventually this practice will help us to be calmer and less reactive in the face of stress—a necessary change if we are to regulate the mind rather than be at its mercy. As we cultivate mindfulness through those forms of Qi Gong that integrate meditation and movement, for example, Pal Dan Gum, we take a quantum leap toward integrating the Buddha's wisdom into our everyday life.

Mindfulness is the essential discipline for training the mind. It requires that we pay close attention to our moment to moment thoughts, feelings, sensations, behavior, fantasies—every aspect of our experience. In short, we must develop a clear awareness of what is happening as we live our lives. This is neither simple nor easy because our mind appears to have a will of its own and because we spend most of our lives on automatic pilot. In being mindful, we make an effort to remain awake so we can practice Qi Gong more effectively. Just as with the breath and the body, regulation of the mind is necessary if we are to attain vibrant health. A trained mind will allow us to see clearly and understand the true nature of our experience. The ability to see clearly and accept the way things are is the spiritual aspect of this practice. It is that which brings balance and harmony to all facets of our lives—not only while we perform Qi Gong movements, but every moment throughout the day. Thus, mindfulness is not just something we practice, it is something that actually changes the way we live our lives.

Mindfulness means making the effort to focus bare attention on what is happening in the here and now. If we want the full benefit of our Qi Gong practice, we must make the effort to focus our awareness on what is actually happening without adding in our personal, idiosyncratic reactions. This strategy concentrates and steadies the mind so we can focus on one thing at a time. This is called one-pointedness, or sometimes single-pointedness. Cultivating one-pointedness is another way we awaken from the dream of ordinary consciousness to become more alive and more aware in our choices. Once we awaken and learn to concentrate, we will be mindful not only of what is happening around us, but within us. In this way, we learn to attend to and observe our internal world of experience without becoming distracted by the endless self-talk and junk that clutters the mind. Thus, mindfulness is a strategy of focusing our attention to concentrate on one thing at a time in order to gain some sense of control over our otherwise untrained mind.

the six robbers and demons of the mind

As we work with them, the demons will enrich our lives. They have been called "manure for enlightenment" or "mind weeds," which we pull up or bury near the plant to give it nourishment.
—JACK KORNFIELD

To a Buddhist, watching one's stream of consciousness is called "guarding against the six robbers." The six robbers are sight, sound, smell, touch, taste, and uncontrolled thoughts. They are, of course, perceptions associated with the eyes, ears, nose, body, tongue, and mind. When we become lost in or attached to our perceptions, regardless whether we judge them as positive or negative, we are robbed of our Buddha nature. This is where the philosophies of Buddhism and Taoism dovetail. A central concept in Taoism is that of stillness, which is not seeing, not hearing, not smelling, not touching, not tasting, and the thought of no thought. Thus, the Taoist who practices stillness in order to stop thought is like the Buddhist who is being mindful of the six robbers in order to stay on the path toward enlightenment.

The robber most likely to undermine our Buddha nature is pollution from thought. This is said to occur when the mind generates some thought that disturbs us emotionally. Buddhists consider the root of all suffering to be emotional attachment or, for that matter, attachment to sensory gratification from sight, sound, smell, touch, or taste. Again, the Taoists agree. The *Tao Te Ching* informs us, "The five colors blind the eye. The five tones deafen the ear. The five flavors dull the taste" (12). To successfully regulate our minds, we must learn not to become too attached to our sensory experiences, however gratifying they may be. This is the idea of detachment. It is crucial in Qi Gong training theory because only by detaching can we control our emotions—a key to preserving health and healing illness. This makes sense because emotions affect the balance and flow of Qi, and Qi exerts the controlling influence on our body and mind.

Mindfulness shows us where and how we get caught up in our emotions. Think of the word emotion ("e-motion") as standing for "energy in motion," then consider how stress and negative emotions harm the body. Using the traditional Oriental model of the meridian system, emotional tension is believed to obstruct the healthy flow of energy by constricting the Qi channels. This is especially true for what the Taoist masters called the demons of the mind (their version of the six robbers). The most destructive of the demons are anger and hatred, prolonged sorrow, and the painful aspects of desire—cravings and addictions of all kinds. In other words, negative emotional experiences create imbalances and blockages in the vast energetic network that flows throughout the human body. It is not easy to control these emotional "demons," but by making space for them in conscious awareness and observing them, we have a way to work with them.

This is what the Buddha intended when he instructed his students to silently note, "This is a mind filled with craving," or "This is a mind filled with rage." By observing our emotions during a meditative state, regardless of whether it is a sitting meditation or a meditation-in-motion such as Pal Dan Gum, we cultivate the quality of mindfulness. This makes it possible to understand our "robbers" and "demons" more fully and balance what is reactive within us. When we observe and name our emotions rather than act them out, we encourage a peacefulness of mind and a stillness of body. On an energetic level, we are maintaining (or restoring) the proper flow and balance of Qi in order to balance and harmonize the fields of energy associated with our minds and bodies. When we stay present-centered we are less likely to interpret what is happening according to negative life experiences that continue to influence our reactions. Because we pay "bare" attention to what is happening to us and around us, we are free to use our emotions as positive energy intended to direct our lives. Emotions that are met with mindfulness are like "arrows" that guide us to behave in more appropriate and satisfying ways.

On the other hand, when we are controlled by our emotions we are always suffering for lack of mindfulness. We simply react without awareness—our bodies tense, our minds wage war, and we tune out our spiritual senses. At times, we become so identified with our emotions we forget who we are and believe we are our emotions. Given enough stress, it is easy to forget we are spiritual beings who also happen to experience emotions. Thus, when we are not being mindful, our "robbers" and "demons" can get control over how we think, feel, and relate, both to ourselves and to others. Mindfulness is a way of balancing the mind regardless of how intense or seductive our emotions are. It allows us to notice what is happening without being so reactive, without judging something or someone as good or bad, without trying to control or avoid the situation at hand. We can then remember who we really are.

Mindfulness is paradoxical. By becoming more awake and attentive to that which distracts or disturbs us, no matter how painful, we develop a different relationship to it and we settle down. This frees us up to "lean into" our emotions and even make friends with them. This is equanimity—the ability to live from our spiritual center and remain even-tempered and "together" under pressure. Equanimity stabilizes the mind while we experience the inevitable changes and stressors of life. Buddhist meditation author Jack Kornfield uses the image of a mountain to illustrate the quality of equanimity. The mountain just sits there regardless of what happens. The sun beats down on it, the rain falls, it gets buried in snow, and struck by bolts of lightning. And what does the mountain do in response to such extremes? It remains unmoved and unwavering! The quality of equanimity is cultivated over time as we practice mindfulness and is considered a key factor in attaining enlightenment. Pal Dan Gum will help us learn to be like the mountain.

pal dan gum as meditation in motion

. . . mindfulness in daily life is important—perhaps central—but it will only go so far without increasing the range of possibilities of the body's behavior (which is achieved through movement and exercises) . . .
—RICHARD SMOLEY

There is an old Tibetan proverb, "It's a tall order to ask for meat without bones, and tea without leaves." This means, among other things, that as long as you have a mind, you will also have distracting thoughts and disturbing emotions. Quite simply, this is why people meditate, which is essentially about being awake and mindful (more about meditation in Chapter 9). Meditation is a way of meeting the "six robbers" and "demons of the mind" as they arise. That they do arise is known by everyone who has attempted to meditate, and this reality will make it necessary to practice mindfulness as you perform Pal Dan Gum— which is a meditation-in-motion. *Even as you concentrate on moving correctly, your mind will want to run away to something more interesting—a task left unfinished, a song playing in your head, a troubled relationship, whether the rain will hurt the rhubarb, or whatever. When this happens, simply notice the distraction without judging it, without grasping it or avoiding it, and return your attention to the sensations of your breathing.* It is this process of combining mindfulness with movement that makes Pal Dan Gum a form of meditation as well as a set of energy exercises.

Training your mind does not mean tuning out your body sensations as you practice the Eight Silken Movements. Pay attention to the internal sensations that accompany each movement as they arise. This will help you to reconnect with your body and feel more at home in it. Try to develop a distinct sensory awareness for each movement—notice how your abdomen expands and contracts as you inhale and exhale, attend to the feeling of tension as you hold the stretches, watch for any areas of muscular soreness or tightness, note any sensory feedback related to balance, experience the pleasure of moving slowly and gracefully. If you find yourself becoming distracted, simply return your attention to the sensations of inhaling and exhaling as you breathe deep into the Dan Tien. By returning awareness to the breath each time you go away in your mind, you will ground yourself and reconnect with the here and now. Eventually this process will focus and steady your powers of concentration and the quality of your Qi Gong practice will improve.

After practicing mindfulness for some time, you may experience an unfamiliar mental state where you are actually not thinking. It may last for an instant or, if you are blessed, for the duration of your Qi Gong routine. The Taoists refer to this as emptiness of mind, or returning to the state of Void. When it occurs, it means you have trained your mind to the point where you are now experiencing "the thought of no thought." This achievement reflects a deep meditative state where the usual contents of the mind have been dismissed from conscious awareness. In the Void, the mind is uncluttered and the body effortlessly and properly breathes itself without mental cueing.

Performing Pal Dan Gum with emptiness of mind is the ultimate goal in training and regulating the mind. It is a blissful feeling of inner quiet—of feeling one with the movements and flowing through the sequence with total freedom. Emptiness of mind is the prize for learning to pay bare attention to the freshness of the present moment—for becoming mindful without judging or being reactive. Even if you only glimpse the Void, cultivating mindfulness will allow you to "untangle the tangle" by listening to and healing your mind and body. Mindfulness will become a way of being in the world, as opposed to something that is done only while meditating or performing Qi Gong. The ability to be mindful is a gift from God. Accept the gift.

chapter 6

A tree as great as a man's embrace springs from a small shoot;
A terrace nine stories high begins with a pile of earth;
A journey of a thousand miles starts under one's feet.
—LAO TZU
Tao Te Ching (64)

Pal Dan Gum

getting started

We learn to do something by doing it. There is no other way.
—JOHN HOLT

This chapter presents some tips for getting started in your practice, followed by the instructions for performing Pal Dan Gum. The format for learning the movements is easy-to-follow. First, you will be given the name of each movement and its starting position. This will be followed by step-by-step directions and photographs showing you how to do the movement from start to finish, and how to breathe properly as the movement proceeds. The health benefits of performing each movement will be explained before the instructions.

Because it is a gentle and flowing meditation-in-motion, Pal Dan Gum offers a safe, natural, and effective approach to healing the body, mind, and spirit. Getting started is easy! Nonetheless, in order to get the maximum benefit from the eight simple but powerful movements that make up Pal Dan Gum, it is best to observe the following guidelines for practice.

Who Can Practice

Pal Dan Gum is beneficial for men and women, regardless of age. Because it is a gentle, virtually no-impact form of exercise that can be practiced at different levels of exertion, it is also suitable for children and the elderly. Pal Dan Gum is appropriate for anyone who suffers from ill health, especially those with chronic conditions. Avoid practicing anytime you feel so ill that rest would be more beneficial than exercise. If you are currently rehabilitating an injury or experiencing a pain condition, please consult your health care professional about these exercises before beginning to practice. Women who are experiencing a heavy menstrual flow are advised to delay practice until the flow has subsided.

Clothing

Simplicity is the key. Wear clothing that is comfortable and won't restrict your freedom and range of movement. Be especially sure to loosen your belt or any constrictive clothing that would interfere with breathing deeply into the Dan Tien. Less clothing is better than more clothing, as long as you are warm enough. Cotton is preferred over other materials because its natural fibers "breathe" and are soft. It is best to go barefoot so the soles of your feet make good contact with the ground. This allows you to "stand like a tree" and feel a better connection with the magnetic field of the earth. If you must wear shoes, choose a pair with thin soles so you can still benefit from the feeling of being rooted.

Place

Whenever possible, practice in the open air, preferably near trees and plants. When weather or circumstances do not allow you to go outdoors, practice indoors in a place that is cool but not cold, well-ventilated but not drafty. Regardless of whether you are outdoors or in, it is best to have your own sacred space for doing Pal Dan Gum and to use that same space every time you practice. Choose a quiet, meditative space that feels nourishing and where you are unlikely to be disturbed.

Time of Day

According to the ancient masters, the best times to do Qi Gong exercises are in the early morning hours and again in the early evening hours, at least one-half hour before supper. If these times don't fit with your schedule, practice whenever it suits you. However, if you are only going to practice Pal Dan Gum once a day, I strongly recommend it be early in the morning. Practice should be done on an empty or half-empty stomach (a full stomach inhibits energy flow) and with an empty bowel and bladder (so you will not feel distracted).

I enjoy practicing first thing in the morning and again in the late evening, just before bedtime. However, some people find that Pal Dan Gum is too energizing and that practicing too close to bedtime causes insomnia or restless sleep. Everyone is different, so experiment and find the time or times that feel most beneficial for you. And remember, Pal Dan Gum takes only six minutes, so you may wish to add extra sessions during moments of spare time. *Make your practice an everyday part of your life, not a daily decision, and never miss two days in a row.*

eight silken movements

The body should be supple like an infant;
the movements should be flexible like a snake;
the feeling should be soft like water;
the breathing should be smooth like a cloud.
—QI GONG PROVERB

The Eight Silken Movements that make up Pal Dan Gum can easily be learned using the following instructions and photographs. Plan to devote about 10-20 minutes to learning each movement (some take a little longer than others). As a beginner, concentrate on first learning the movement, then the proper breathing pattern. Learn the movements in the correct sequence, since they are always practiced in the same order. After learning Movement I, move on to Movement II, and so on. You will get the maximum benefits if you keep in mind the following guidelines:

1. *Refer to the instructional photographs frequently.* Before beginning, read through all eight movements to get an overview. Then, before trying a movement, carefully read all the notes and instructions for that move. Think of the photographs as a private lesson from an experienced teacher who is providing ongoing supervision. Study each photograph carefully and, if possible, check your form in a full-length mirror to ensure you are practicing correctly. Refinement will come with practice, but it is best to begin your practice with good form so you don't have to unlearn a mistake or a bad habit later. Pal Dan Gum, like all forms of active Qi Gong, is meant to be done with precision.

This means using correct posture, keeping your spinal column straight (except for Movement VI which calls for arching your back), shifting your weight evenly as you move from one stance to another, always maintaining your balance, and flowing smoothly from one movement to the next. By consulting the photographs frequently, you are more likely to develop and refine these elements of good form.

Note that each photograph is identified by a roman numeral indicating which of the eight movements is being demonstrated, and an Arabic numeral indicating its order in the series of photographs demonstrating that particular movement. Thus, Figure II-1 is a demonstration of Movement II and is the first (starting position) in the series of photographs demonstrating that particular movement; Figure VIII-3 is a demonstration of Movement VIII, third in the series of photographs demonstrating that movement. At the end of each movement, there is a sequence of photographs showing the entire movement and its proper breathing.

2. *Relax and move slowly.* Before you begin Movement I, take a moment to stand with correct posture, relax your body, and root yourself to feel grounded. This will ensure your movements are natural and relaxed, thus opening the Qi channels to facilitate the free flow of energy that is necessary for vibrant health. Remind yourself that Pal Dan Gum is intended to be done slowly and deliberately from start to finish. This is not only good form, it makes it easier to learn the different steps of each movement and to avoid making careless mistakes. With the exception of Movement VII, *Punching With Angry Eyes,* you should feel as though you are performing the entire sequence of movements in slow motion (but not too slowly).

Slow movement helps relax your body and mind so you can flow smoothly from one movement to the next—as if you were "pulling silk from a cocoon." It will also help you stay in balance throughout the sequence of movements (this is a fundamental principle in all schools of Qi Gong training). In terms of Qi Gong training theory, Pal Dan Gum is considered a "soft way" of exercising and balancing your energy. This means you should never harm your body through excessive effort or a hurried pace. If you are physically unable to do any part of a movement, simply adapt that movement by approximating it as best you can. As you become stronger or better coordinated you will improve your ability and form. Remember, Pal Dan Gum is intended to promote strength and health through slow movement, relaxed stretching, and regular practice.

3. *Stretch to less than full capacity.* All stretching during Pal Dan Gum should be done to something less than full capacity. Stretch to a point where

you feel mild to moderate tension in the muscles that are being stretched. For most people this will be about 70 to 85 percent of capacity (a bit more for those who already have some flexibility, a bit less for those who are less flexible). Err on the side of making easy stretches and then gradually, over a period of days or weeks, go a fraction of an inch further. *Stretching slowly lengthens muscle and teaches the body to move through its full range of motion. Increased flexibility comes from holding each stretch and really relaxing into it, not from straining to the utmost.* Trying to force a tight or contracted muscle to stretch too far is a stretching taboo because it will only cause it to contract even tighter. A good rule of thumb is to ease off if you feel more than mild to moderate tension during any stretch, and stop if you experience any pain.

Do not lock your joints, which restricts the free flow of Qi, and do not bounce! Bouncing is a type of "ballistic" stretching where one attempts to further stretch a muscle by making quick and repeated little jerking movements while already in a stretched position. This gives the illusion of furthering a stretch but it actually signals the muscle it is being stretched too far, causing the muscle to contract and tighten itself for protection against injury. Bouncing takes you too close to 100 percent stretching capacity and is thus counterproductive because it risks injury to your muscles, tendons, and ligaments. It can also tear the fascia (the thin layer of soft connective tissue that binds our muscles together), resulting in scar tissue and further loss of flexibility.

Pal Dan Gum calls for slow and deliberate "static" stretches. Static stretching is a method where a muscle is placed in a stretched position, then held for a second or two in order that it elongate beyond its normal length. A static stretch is a safe approach to stretching because it signals the muscle to let go and lengthen. The beneficial effect of this approach is paradoxical—by stretching to less than full capacity and holding that position, you develop longer muscles and full range flexibility. For those who participate in athletics, this method of slow s-t-r-e-t-c-h-i-n-g will build strength and stamina, improve coordination, relieve soreness and pain, and reduce the risk of injury.

4. *Remember to breathe properly.* Keep in mind the three keys to regulating your breath pattern: slender, silent, and deep. This means you inhale slowly and quietly through your nostrils, drawing the breath deep down into your abdomen, pause momentarily, then make a thorough exhalation through your nostrils, pause momentarily before the next inhalation, and continue the pattern. Try to coordinate your breathing and body movements as you perform Pal Dan Gum. Usually this means beginning your inhalation as you begin a movement, pausing your breath momentarily as you hold a stretch, then beginning your exhalation as you begin your return to the starting position, where you

pause momentarily before beginning the next movement and inhalation. The correct breathing pattern for each movement is shown in the sequence photographs at the end of the movement. Don't worry about getting this down and breathing properly until you have practiced for several months. If you do nothing other than breathe deep down into the Dan Tien you will have significantly improved your breath pattern.

5. *Expectations:* Do not expect yourself to learn the entire sequence of movements or proper breathing in one session. No one becomes a Qi Gong master in a few months or even a few years of practice. There is an old saying, "You don't learn to play the cello in a week!" This holds true for Qi Gong. Be patient with yourself and keep an eye out for any negative judgments about how fast or how well you are learning the movements. If you are being impatient or self-critical, just notice that with mindfulness and gently return your attention to the sensations of your breathing pattern. Pal Dan Gum is really quite simple. You will learn it fast enough if you follow the guidelines and practice regularly.

Do have positive expectations of what Pal Dan Gum can do for you. Whatever your expectations are, whatever you wanted for yourself when you decided to buy or read this book, expect that you will be fulfilled. There is a part of you, a healer within, that knows you can heal any problems of the body, mind, and spirit. *Given regular practice and sufficient time, these powerful exercises can strengthen and harmonize your energy field and restore your body to its genetic memory of wellness.* Pal Dan Gum is an ancient and proven way of tapping into your own healing potential, as well as the unlimited healing energy that is always available through God. There is only one thing to do—imagine yourself vibrantly healthy and expect the desired changes to happen!

6. *Warming up:* As with other forms of exercise, warming up is a good idea, especially if you have areas of bodily tension or discomfort. Because the Eight Silken Movements are gentle and the stretches are done to less than full capacity, warming up need not take more than a minute or two—unless you choose otherwise. Begin the warm-up by scanning your body top to bottom, inside and out, while paying close attention to how it feels. With careful mindfulness, notice any places that feel tight or sore, or where your energy feels blocked. Breathe positive Qi into areas of discomfort and release negative Qi as you breathe out. Now, rub your hands together to generate heat and briskly massage any and all areas of discomfort. This is called "An Mo Gong," which means "massage work" or "self-massage." It has been used for centuries in the Orient to awaken the Qi and begin the process of opening the channels through which energy flows.

Another technique is to make a loose fist with each hand and gently tap/tap your entire body with either the front or the backs of your hands (tapping with the front or palm of your closed hand is easiest on the front of your body, and vice versa). Be sure to tap/tap all around the Dan Tien area, front and back, as well as any areas that are in need of healing. To me, gentle tap/tapping feels best for awakening the Qi and rubbing best to open the Qi channels, so I do both. You can also roll your shoulders, flex your knees, and swing your hips as you tap/tap and rub your body. This will loosen up the major joints of your body to get the Qi moving through these important areas. When you feel sufficiently warmed up, begin the sequence of movements and really relax into each stretch, especially those that involve a particular area of discomfort.

With these guidelines in mind, you are ready to practice Pal Dan Gum!

Upholding heaven with both hands

Health Benefits: *Upholding Heaven With Both Hands* prepares you for the next seven movements by invigorating the muscles and relaxing the body as a whole. It improves posture by bringing the body's segments (head, shoulders, thorax, pelvis, legs) into a more vertical alignment. It opens and balances the Qi channels to increase blood circulation, improve digestion, and promote deeper respiration. This exercise also stimulates the endocrine system to enhance sexual functioning.

I.1 Stand erect, with the top of your head reaching upward, chin slightly tucked.

- Your feet are shoulder-width apart.
- Your arms are at your sides, hands together just below your navel, palms up, fingers interlaced.
- Eyes forward.

¹.2 Inhale slowly and deeply.

- Separate your fingers and raise your arms slowly away from your sides.

Note: your inhalation is one deep breath from movement I.2 to I.4

I.3 Fingers meet above your head.

   • Interlace your fingers, palms down.

I.4 Rotate your palms up to face the sky, and stretch your arms with effort until your elbows are fully extended.

  • Go up on your toes and hold the stretch 1-2 seconds.

I.5 Exhale slowly and thoroughly, slowly lower your heels, and float your arms back to your sides.

Repeat the sequence 2 more times, raising your arms 3 times in all.

movement I sequence

inhale

Note: If you lose your balance when you go up on your toes, move your feet farther apart in the starting position. By widening your base you will find it easier to maintain your balance. Then, as your balance improves over time, gradually move your feet back to shoulder-width apart. Notice that the starting position for Movement I and, for that matter, for all of the eight movements, is only slightly different from Standing Like a Tree, the "posture of power," shown on page 35.

exhale

Drawing the bow with each hand

Health Benefits: *Drawing The Bow With Each Hand* increases the capacity and resiliency of the lungs for proper breathing. It stimulates the heart and improves blood circulation. It also strengthens the muscles of the arms, shoulders, chest, and thighs. This exercise builds and balances the Qi that flows throughout the whole body to enhance immune function.

II.1 Flowing smoothly from Movement I, step to the left, placing your feet slightly wider apart than your shoulders.

- Bend your knees to the point of exertion (horse-riding position).
- Cross your arms in front of your chest, tucking your right arm under your left arm.
- Your right hand is in a loose fist, thumb touching your index finger, as if holding a bowstring.
- Your left index finger points skyward.
- Eyes forward.

II.2 Inhale slowly and deeply.

- Push your left arm slowly to the left until your elbow is fully extended (as if drawing a bow).
- At same time, pull your right arm slowly to the right with the elbow bent (as if pulling a bowstring).
- Eyes follow your left index finger so that your head turns left as the bow opens.
- Hold the stretch several seconds.

II.3 Exhale slowly and thoroughly as you float your arms back to the front of your chest, tucking your left arm under your right.

- Your left hand is in a loose fist, thumb touching your index finger.
- Your right index finger points skyward.

II.4 Inhale slowly and deeply.

- Push your right arm slowly to the right until your elbow is extended (drawing the bow).
- At the same time, pull your left arm slowly to the left with your elbow bent (pulling the bowstring).
- Eyes follow your right index finger so that your head turns right as the bow opens.
- Hold the stretch several seconds.

II.5 Exhale and float your arms back into the crossed position, with your right arm again tucked under your left.

Repeat the sequence 2 more times, alternating until you draw the bow 3 times to each side.

movement II sequence

inhale   exhale

Note: Maintain horse riding position and keep your weight balanced throughout Movement II. This will help you develop a strong root so you feel grounded and stable on your feet. Imagine you are intending to shoot the arrow a long distance and that the finger that points is aimed at your target. Hence, as you draw the bow open, the hand that holds the bow-string should be lower than the hand that holds the bow (notice the upward aim in Figures II-2 and II-4).

inhale

exhale

Raising the hands one at a time

Health Benefits: *Raising The Hands One At A Time* adjusts and regulates the functions of the stomach to improve digestion and aids the process of elimination. It increases Qi circulation to the spleen to enhance immune function. This exercise stretches all the muscles of the rib cage to increase lung capacity and strengthens the chest, upper back, shoulders, and arms. It also benefits the liver and gall bladder.

III.1 Step smoothly from the horse-riding position (Movement II) to stand erect with your feet shoulder-width apart.

- Arms at your sides, hands together just below your navel, palms up, fingers interlaced.
- Eyes forward.

III.2 Inhale slowly and deeply.

- Separate your fingers and push your left hand above the crown of your head, palm up, until your elbow is fully extended.
- At the same time, push your right hand below your tailbone, palm down, until the elbow is fully extended.
- Hold the stretch several seconds.

III.3 Exhale slowly and thoroughly as you relax and return to the starting position with fingers interlaced.

III.4 Inhale slowly and deeply.

- Separate your fingers and push your right hand above the crown of your head, palm up, until your elbow is fully extended.
- At the same time, push your left hand below your tailbone, palm down, until the elbow is fully extended.
- Hold the stretch several seconds.

III.5 Exhale slowly and thoroughly as you relax and return again to the starting position, with fingers interlaced.

Repeat the sequence 2 more times, alternating raising the left and right hands 3 times on each side.

movement III sequence

inhale   exhale

Note: Your hands should be pushed up and down with effort to ensure maximum health benefits. As always, stretch to something less than full capacity and gradually extend your stretches as you gain flexibility.

inhale

exhale

Turning the head and looking behind

Health Benefits: *Turning The Head And Looking Behind* is an exercise that energizes and tones the central nervous system—the brain and spinal cord. It is said to cure the "five troubles and seven disorders" by rejuvenating internal organs, increasing immune function, and promoting emotional well-being. The "five troubles" are eye strain due to overuse, and muscle strains caused by too much lying, sitting, standing, and walking. The "seven disorders" refer to physical symptoms caused by fear, rage, distress, overeating, exhaustion, chills, and extreme climates. Movement IV also prevents neck problems by increasing the strength and flexibility of the muscles of the neck. It is a wonderful antidote to the rounded upper back, forward head, and collapsed chest posture that too often comes with the process of aging.

IV.1 Remain standing erect, with your feet shoulder-width apart.

- Cross your arms in front of your chest, folding your left arm over your right.
- Eyes forward.

IV.2 Inhale slowly and deeply as you expand your chest and stretch your arms down and away from your body, palms facing skyward.

- At the same time, turn your upper body and head to the left and look backward over your left shoulder as far as possible.
- Hold your stretch several seconds.

IV.3 Exhale slowly and thoroughly as you let your arms float slowly back to the folded position, this time folding your right arm over your left.

IV.4 Inhale slowly as you expand your chest and stretch your arms down and away from your body, palms facing up.

- At the same time, turn your upper body and head to the right and look backward over your right shoulder as far as possible.
- Hold your stretch several seconds.

IV.5 Exhale slowly as your arms float back to the folded position, with left arm over the right again.

Repeat the sequence 2 more times, alternating looking left and right, for a total of 3 times to each side.

movement IV sequence

inhale   exhale

Note: To ensure the maximum benefit from Movement IV, remember to draw the breath way down into the Dan Tien as you inhale. Remember, when your left arm is folded over your right, you turn to the left, and vice versa. As you turn your upper body and head in tandem, your spinal column rotates but remains straight up and down; do not sway or arch your back.

inhale

exhale

Bending the trunk and stretching the neck

Health Benefits: *Bending The Trunk And Stretching The Neck* is said to "tranquilize the fiery heart." The ancient practitioners of Pal Dan Gum would "bend to the four directions" to extinguish "fire" (stress and tension) which accumulated in the heart. Excessive fire causes symptoms such as headache, insomnia, agitation, rage reactions, and high blood pressure—symptoms that plague modern man. Movement V also increases the flexibility of the spine and strengthens the low back, hips, and thighs. The neck stretches will strengthen and relax your neck by lengthening the muscles that connect head, neck, and shoulders. Because these neck movements are anatomically harmless, any significant discomfort or pain is indicative of a pre-existing problem. In such a case, consult with a physician or qualified health care practitioner.

V.1 Flow smoothly into this move by stepping to the left so your feet are slightly wider than shoulder-width.

- Bend your knees to the point of exertion (horse-riding position).
- Place your hands on your hips and keep them there, thumbs on the backside of your body, fingers in front.
- Eyes forward.

Bending The Trunk

V.2 Inhale slowly while bending your trunk sideways to the left with effort.
- Hold your stretch several seconds.
- Exhale slowly and float back up to the starting position.

V.3 Inhale slowly while bending your trunk sideways to the right with effort.

    • Hold your stretch several seconds.

    • Exhale slowly and float back up to the starting position.

V.4 Inhale slowly and bend forward until you are looking between your legs.

- Hold your position several seconds.
- Exhale slowly and, *using your legs*, slowly lift back to the starting position.

V.5 Inhale slowly and arch gently backwards *without straining your lower back*, pulling your head and shoulders back as your chest expands up and out.

   • Hold your position several seconds.

V.6 Exhale slowly and float back up to the starting position.

Repeat the sequence 2 more times—bending left, right, forward, and backward a total of 3 times in each direction. Keep your head, neck, and spine in a straight line.

Stretching the Neck

While maintaining the starting (horse-riding) position, continue with the next part of Movement V.

V.7 Inhale slowly, and gently stretch your head to the left, so your left ear moves toward your left shoulder.

> • Exhale slowly, and gently return your head to the upright position.

V.8 Inhale slowly, and gently stretch your head to the right, so your right ear moves toward your right shoulder.

> • Exhale slowly, and gently return your head to the upright position.

V.9 Inhale and slowly stretch your head forward so your chin goes toward your chest, touching it, if possible.

  • Exhale slowly, and gently return your head to the upright position.

V.10 Inhale slowly, and gently bend your head backward so your chin points skyward.

    • Exhale and slowly return your head to its upright position.

Repeat the sequence 2 more times—left ear to shoulder, right ear to shoulder, chin down, chin up—for a total of 3 times in each direction.

Note: Keep your jaw relaxed throughout the neck stretches and remember to stretch to less than full capacity. Let your shoulders drop and be sure not to lift them on the shoulder to ear movements. Traditional Pal Dan Gum teaches a head-rolling movement during Movement V (as do many other Qi Gong and stretching routines). However, because your neck joints do not have a ball-and-socket configuration, rolling your head around on your neck can cause or worsen degenerative joint disease. The neck stretching movements suggested here eliminate neck-rolling and thus honor the limitations of your anatomy.

movement V sequence

bending the trunk

exhale

inhale

exhale

inhale →

stretching the neck

exhale

inhale

exhale

inhale →

exhale   inhale   exhale   inhale

exhale   inhale   exhale   inhale

Touching the toes and arching the back

Caution: *If you experience lower back problems, do not perform this exercise until a qualified health care professional has approved these movements for you.*

Health Benefits: *Touching The Toes And Arching The Back* opens the Qi channels responsible for nourishing the internal organs of the body, especially benefiting the kidneys and adrenal glands. It also improves the flexibility and strength of the lower back, waist, and hip joints.

VI.1 Flow smoothly into this move by stepping out of horse-riding position so that your feet are shoulder-width apart.

- Stand erect, arms relaxed at your sides.
- Eyes forward.

VI.2 Inhale slowly and deeply.

- Bend forward and pinch the sides of your big toes or grab your ankles.
- *Bend your knees, if necessary, in order not to strain your lower back.*
- Hold your position several seconds.

VI.3 Exhale slowly.

- Bend your knees and, using your legs, slowly lift yourself back to the starting position.
- Place the palms of your hands over your kidneys, at about the level of the lowest ribs in your back.

VI.4 Inhale slowly and deeply.

- Arch your body and bend backward until you feel a good stretch but *without straining your lower back*.
- Hold your position for several seconds.

VI.5 Exhale slowly and gently return to the starting position.
Repeat the sequence 2 more times, bending forward and back a total of 3 times.

movement VI sequence

inhale

exhale

inhale   exhale

Punching with angry eyes

Health Benefits: *Punching With Angry Eyes* is designed to build physical strength in the legs, arms, and upper back. It also strengthens the life force and revitalizes the inner organs, especially the liver and heart. Through the discharge of pent-up, negative emotional energy such as frustration and anger, this exercise adjusts the Qi to return the mind and body to a state of balance. The emphasis on glaring with angry eyes is a technique handed down by the ancient Qi Gong masters. It is intended to focus concentration and raise up the Shen, that is, cultivate the spiritual power that guides us.

VII.I Flow smoothly into this movement by stepping to the left so your feet are wider apart than your shoulders.

- Bend your knees to the point of exertion (horse-riding position).
- Make your eyes wide and on fire with anger.
- Make an angry grimace, baring clenched teeth.
- Clench your fists and hold them into your chest, about breast high.

VII.2 Inhale slowly and rotate your trunk to the left.

   • Throw a punch with your left arm and fist, exhaling with an angry
     sound on the punch.

VII.3 Then throw a punch with your right arm and fist, continuing your exhale with an angry sound.

VII.4 Rotate to face forward.

> • Inhale slowly and then throw two more punches, first with the left
>   arm and fist, exhaling with an angry sound on the punches.

VII.5 Then throw a punch with your right arm and fist, continuing the long exhale with an angry sound.

VII.6 Inhale slowly and rotate your trunk to the right.

> • Throw two more punches, first with the left arm and fist, exhaling with an angry sound on the punches.

VII.7 Throw a punch with your right arm and fist, again continuing your exhale with an angry sound.

> • Inhale slowly and rotate your trunk to the left again.

Repeat the sequence two more times, doing 18 punches in all (6 to the left, 6 to the center, 6 to the right).

movement VII sequence

inhale

exhale

exhale

exhale

Note: Gather your energy as you inhale, then discharge that energy as you throw each punch. As you throw punches, imagine you are a striking snake. Make a hissing, spitting sound by expelling air through your teeth. Movement VII is not a martial art exercise to develop punching power. Rather, throw your punches with deliberation and never so hard as to twist or stress your spinal column or arms. Keep the fire in your eyes throughout this exercise and have the feeling of ventilating any blocked anger. Do not direct your angry energy at any person or any other living thing.

Raising the heels to keep all illnesses away

Health Benefits: It seems fitting to end Pal Dan Gum with an exercise that is designed to maintain vibrant health. *Raising The Heels To Keep All Illnesses Away* was considered by the ancients to prevent illness by strengthening both mind and body. It is intended to strengthen the Qi flow to the spine and brain and is believed to massage the internal organs. Although this exercise cannot guarantee a life free from illness, gently jolting the body does stimulate the reflexes on the soles of the feet. This is similar to the method of reflexology in stimulating key acupoints to relieve nervous tension and activate the body's healing potentials. It also relieves pain throughout the body, especially that resulting from poor posture. Pushing up on the toes and holding the position one second (two if possible) will dramatically strengthen the ankles and calf muscles, thus preventing many common sports injuries, for example, ankle sprains, leg cramps, and shin splints.

VIII.1 Flow smoothly into Movement VIII by stepping out of horse-riding position and standing erect.

- Reach upward with the top of your head.
- Draw your chin in slightly.
- Pull your shoulders back slightly.
- Gently press your palms against your thighs.
- Feet shoulder-width apart.

VIII.2 Inhale deeply and raise your heels as high as possible by pushing up on your toes.

- Hold your breath and position a second or two.
- Lower your heels so that you give your body a gentle, low-impact jolt as you come down.

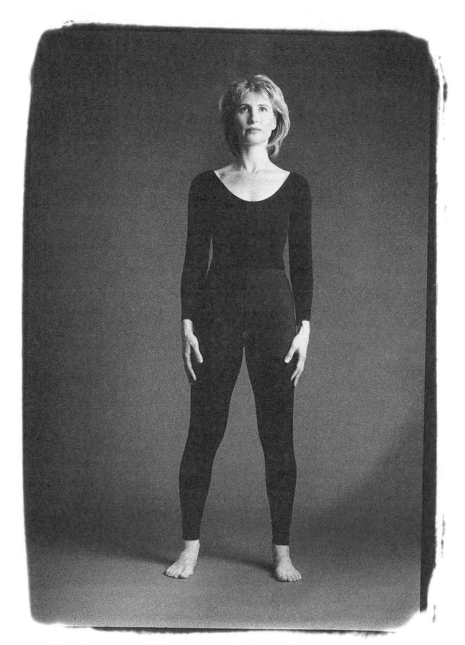

VIII.3 Complete your exhalation as you return to the starting position.

Repeat the sequence 9 more times, raising your heels 10 times in all.

movement VIII sequence

inhale   exhale

Note: There isn't time to take the usual long and slow breath during this movement, so concentrate on inhaling deep into the Dan Tien and making each breath uniform. In my own practice, I have modified Movement VIII to keep my eyes closed throughout; however, this is optional. By keeping your eyes closed, you learn to ground yourself with your feet and the base of your body as nature intends, rather than using your eyes. This will promote a stronger and more developed root system—an important aspect of body regulation. Experiment by practicing this exercise first with your eyes open, then closed. You will notice it is much easier to keep your balance with your eyes open because you are grounding yourself with your eyes; however, this reinforces being too much "in your head." If you are having difficulty keeping your balance when you raise your heels, with or without your eyes closed, widen your stance in the starting position until you can remain balanced for all ten repetitions. Then, as your balance improves over time, gradually move your feet closer together. Remember to keep your knees soft and slightly flexed so they can function as shock absorbers for your body.

Congratulations! You have completed the Eight Silken Movements. If you wish, place your palms together below your chin and bow respectfully to express gratitude to the ancient masters who originated these simple but powerful exercises.

chapter 7

People usually fail when they are on the verge of success.
So give as much care to the end as to the beginning
Then there will be no failure.
　　—LAO TZU
　　　Tao Te Ching (64)

Practicing Well!

In the Spring of 1990, I spent several days at a Zen Buddhist monastery in Santa Fe, New Mexico. On the way out of the parking lot, a sign read "Practice Well!" This simple suggestion struck me as profound and still serves to remind me that I will get out of my practice what I put into it.

Qi Gong is referred to as a "practice" because it is to be done on a daily basis and because it is to be performed repeatedly to acquire and polish certain skills. For our purposes, practicing well means wearing loose fitting and comfortable clothing, choosing a meditative space to practice, and making practice an everyday part of your life. It means using correct posture and form, relaxing and rooting your body, stretching to less than full capacity, and taking slender, silent, deep breaths as you perform each movement. By practicing well I affirm that Pal Dan Gum is more than just a set of exercises—it is a healing and spiritual art passed down to us through many generations of Qi Gong masters. As with other types of energy training, Pal Dan Gum provides a way to approach the whole of life with health, balance, and harmony.

Mastering Pal Dan Gum will take time and self-discipline. This means you must make yourself a "disciple" by practicing regularly with mindfulness and steady effort. The *Tao Te Ching* (41) teaches the same lesson when it tells us the wise student learns the natural way to be and "practices it diligently." Again, we make practicing a part of our everyday life, not something we decide each day if we are going to do or not. We can cultivate self-discipline and refine our technique by not allowing ourselves to miss practice two days in a row. This is easy enough because Pal Dan Gum takes only six minutes from start to finish. If you wish to master Pal Dan Gum and receive its many benefits, you must practice regularly and practice well. We learn Pal Dan Gum the same way we learn to play the piano or excel at a sport—with lots of quality practice.

If you find yourself wanting a longer or more strenuous practice session, there are several ways to modify the usual routine. The easiest is to add repetitions to each of the Eight Silken Movements (double the repetitions for a twelve minute session, triple them for eighteen minutes). Another possibility is to hold the static stretches for a longer period of time. Instead of the usual second or two, you can hold each stretch anywhere from five to twenty seconds, but no longer. If you hold the stretches, inhale slowly as you begin the movement, hold your breath as you hold the stretch, then exhale slowly as you return to the starting position. This is a wonderful way to develop greater flexibility, assuming you are stretching to less than full capacity and really relaxing into each stretch. It is also an ideal way to warm up for or cool down from other athletic activities. If you simply want more practice using the regular routine, increase your number of practice sessions to two or three times a day. Remember, it is better to practice well once a day than to do the movements incorrectly ten times a day.

On the other hand, if you are time-poor and need to squeeze a two-minute practice into a busy schedule, do a short form of Pal Dan Gum by doing each movement once. For example, if you were performing Movement II, you would "draw the bow" once to the left and once to the right; to do Movement V, you would bend the trunk one time to the left, right, forward, and back; then stretch the neck one time to the left, right, forward, and back. A two minute session is not sufficient to awaken the Qi, but long enough to stretch, relax, and rejuvenate your tired muscles. It is also possible to perform one particular exercise for a particular reason. For instance, Movement IV (*Turning The Head and Looking Behind*) is a potent energizer, so if you need to boost your energy level you can simply do ten to twenty repetitions. Or, if you are feeling frustrated or angry for some reason, you might do ten repetitions of Movement VII (*Punching With Angry Eyes*) to discharge negative energy and return to a state of emotional balance.

Practicing well requires awareness of the body and the senses. Each time you do Pal Dan Gum, be aware of any areas of physical discomfort. These are usually *not* indicative of problems requiring consultation with a health care advisor. They are more likely to be physical manifestations of accumulated stress and psychological pain, held in and expressed through the language of the body. For example, a tight sensation in your jaw may mean you are holding in resentment or repressed anger. Shoulders held up and tight often means you are holding anxiety or fear without even knowing it. Part of the healing process is to open up to and notice such patterns of blocked energy or tension, then allow these blockages to release and dissolve away. This will happen spontaneously as you practice Pal Dan Gum because each movement gets the energy flowing freely through a different part of your body. However, if a pain condition develops or worsens, by all means consult with a health care professional before continuing. In this regard, practicing well means paying attention and then exercising good judgment and self-care.

Practicing well also requires awareness of the mind and its experience. As a meditation-in-motion and a spiritual discipline, Pal Dan Gum asks you to accept whatever comes up during practice or around the issue of practice. Acceptance does not mean approval—you don't have to like what comes up— just accept it by letting it in and making space for it. Then, if you fall prey to impatience ("When will I get this movement right?") or the painful aspect of desire ("If only this pain would go away, I could be happy!"), simply notice your thought or feeling without judgment. This holds true for any experience that might interfere with practice—whether it is boredom, doubt, disappointment, or whatever. This is not a "don't push the river" philosophy that says you must be patient or detached—it is one that cultivates awareness by encouraging you to notice when you are "pushing the river." So simply notice what arises, make space for it, allow it to come and go, and know that whatever comes next will be largely determined by how you handle what is happening in the present moment. It is truly not what arises as we practice or even as we live our life, it is how we meet what arises.

Practice does not make perfect. Rather, practicing well makes permanent the benefits of your practice. The key is to practice well every time you do Pal Dan Gum. You will know you are practicing well if during or immediately after doing Pal Dan Gum you feel any or all of the following:

- a pleasant warmth associated with relaxation
- a secure sensation of being more rooted to the ground
- greater clarity or tranquillity of mind
- feeling more alive, aware, or energized

Practicing well means it is better to do one movement with proper breathing and correct execution of the body movements than to perform the entire sequence sloppily. As you practice over time you will gradually refine your performance and get the maximum benefit from your training. You can expect to notice some of the benefits of Pal Dan Gum after the very first practice session, for example relieving muscular tension and emotional stress. Other benefits, such as improved respiration and immune function, will take a little longer. Don't be discouraged if it takes a month or two to notice lasting structural changes in postural alignment. Pal Dan Gum works wonders. Practice well and you will see for yourself.

chapter 8

When positive or joyous feelings and attitudes pass through each organ and circulate through our whole system, our physical and chemical energies are transformed and balanced.
— TARTHANG TULKU

The warrior doesn't try to cast out fear. Instead, fear is regarded as a fat kindling log with which to build a gigantic fire of fearlessness.
— CYNTHIA KNEEN

Self-Healing With Pal Dan Gum

That I have successfully used Pal Dan Gum to recover from a life-threatening illness is one reason I want to share this powerful healing art with everyone. In 1978, about one year before I was introduced to Pal Dan Gum, I developed cancer of the lymph system. I was misdiagnosed when I first reported my symptoms, and the cancer had spread throughout my body by the time an accurate diagnosis was made two years later. Learning that I had lymphoma shattered both my self-concept and body-image. One day I was a 35-year-old competitive marathon runner in seemingly perfect health and the next day I was a cancer patient with a death sentence. I say that because my doctor informed me I had five years to live. Maximum!

I fired that doctor because I was afraid his attitude might be contagious. The truth is he frightened me, and I don't believe fear is good medicine. I found a cancer specialist who understood how the mind and spirit influence the body and who saw modern medicine and self-healing as complementary. I underwent aggressive chemotherapy and the cancer went into remission, but only for one year—then the tumors reappeared. This time I was given a less aggressive form of chemotherapy and again the cancer went into remission—but once more the tumors reappeared in about one year. At that time, one tumor in my neck had grown to the size of an apricot.

With my doctor's permission, I chose to put off further treatment, which would have meant still more chemotherapy and/or radiation treatments. Instead, I focused my efforts on self-healing and took a "wait and see" approach. I decided to make Pal Dan Gum a major part of my healing regimen and to take my practice more seriously. I made a commitment to follow the guidelines I have outlined in this book. I never missed a morning or evening session. I improved my technique by really concentrating on breathing properly, performing the body movements correctly, relaxing into the stretches, and by having positive expectations of being restored to vibrant health. I prayed that I would be filled with healing energy and that I would become a "warrior" with a brave and open heart.

By renewing my commitment to practicing well, Pal Dan Gum came alive as a true meditation-in-motion and spiritual practice. Before, due to my lack of mindfulness, it had been little more than a set of exercises. Now I became more attentive to and less judgmental of what was happening in the present moment. Every moment became an opportunity to live a spiritual life—the way I breathed, the way I held my body and moved, the way I related to others. Qi Gong woke me up and I began to practice living in harmony with myself and the world around me. This put me in a better position to accept the imperfections of life and be more at peace with the way things were, including my illness and the distressing feelings it generated.

I began to see my illness as less of a crisis and more of a challenge—not just to heal physically, but an opportunity to become more of a person and more of who I really was. I thought of my cancer as a wake-up call or, as Bernie Siegel calls it, "God's reset button." I realized I needed to become more open and more loving to myself and others. This was not an easy change to make. At times life seemed too much and I would feel overwhelmed and overburdened with negative emotions. I would certainly have never chosen to have cancer, but the cold reality was that I was seriously ill and could die. The question was not "Why me?" but "What now?" Pal Dan Gum gave me a way to respond to the challenge by cultivating a wholeness of mind, body, and spirit. It allowed me to marshal my self-healing energies and make my body an inhospitable place for cancer cells to survive. My daily practice reconnected me with my body and this helped my body heal itself. Pal Dan Gum became a path of awakening and healing.

Although I felt hopeful much of the time, waiting for my next checkup was very difficult. I found myself obsessing about my illness rather than just living my life. If cancer was a life lesson, I was learning my faith needed to be stronger. I developed a nervous habit of compulsively checking my tumors by measuring them with my fingertips. I did this many times a day and, although they didn't seem to be growing, they didn't seem to be shrinking either. I couldn't eliminate the fear that I might die a cancerous death, and I was undermining my effort to heal by constantly checking myself. Looking back, I was trying to make healing happen rather than getting out of the way and allowing it to happen—trusting it to happen!

Fortunately, each of us has an innate intelligence or inner healer that intuitively knows when we are in our own way, and I knew I could not heal as long as I continued to worry myself sick with these daily inspections. I decided to stop checking and let my doctor tell me how I was doing at my next appointment. This decision proved to be easier said than done. No matter how distressing it was to check for and find cancerous tumors living in my body, it was very difficult not to do it. I especially wanted to feel and measure the large tumor in my neck, and I often had to mentally restrain myself from doing so. Nevertheless, I managed to win the struggle and I actually went without checking for two months—until the night before my scheduled checkup.

What happened that night was the most awesome and defining moment of my life. Driving home from work, I found my fingers touching the right side of my neck, feeling for the large tumor. The last time I had checked, it was the length of my index, middle and ring fingertips combined (over 2 inches long). I rationalized that my doctor would be examining me tomorrow and a few more hours of not checking wouldn't make any difference. To my utter amazement, the tumor was gone. Not smaller, but gone! I quickly checked the other areas of my body where tumors had developed, especially my armpits and groin. Nothing! Just fleshy, healthy-feeling, wonderfully soft lymph nodes. I was so happy and full of gratitude I thought I might burst before getting home to tell my wife. I remember flying down the freeway shouting . . . "Thank you God! Thank you God! Thank you God!" It was miraculous, so it must have been a miracle!

I went for my checkup the next day. My doctor greeted me with his usual and welcomed sense of humor by asking, "How're your lumps and bumps?" I didn't answer. Instead, I asked him to check me over and tell me what *he* thought. First he checked my neck, a logical place to start because it had been the site of the largest tumor. He looked puzzled. Then, very carefully and thoroughly, he examined the rest of my body, taking his time, apparently finding nothing abnormal. His puzzled expression gave way to a look of excitement and then a delighted smile. I will never forgot what he said. It was, "I don't know *what* you're doing, *but keep doing it!*" We talked for awhile, giving the moment its due, and finally he said goodbye and left the room. Left alone, I wept tears of relief and joy, and I heard him dictating a report from across the hall. I remember that he stopped mid-sentence and then, a few moments later, he re-entered the examining room. This time he said, "I'd like to shake your hand!" I know he was really happy for me and I think he was also totally baffled. Words are inadequate to express how blessed and how grateful I felt at that moment and every day since. I felt like I'd won an enormous lotto prize against all odds—only instead of being paid off with money, I got to keep my life!

I cannot prove that Pal Dan Gum healed my cancer because my self-healing strategy was to cover all bases. By that I mean I used a wide range of approaches to bring about healing—physical, psychological, and spiritual. What I can say is that Pal Dan Gum was an integral part of my healing regimen because it is in itself a way of covering the bases. As a physical approach, each of the Eight Silken Movements unblocks the Qi channels to nourish the body's cell tissue and restore a state of vibrant health. As a psychological approach, Pal Dan Gum initiates self-healing by instilling an attitude of positive expectation and promoting deep relaxation in the body and mind. As a spiritual approach and meditation-in-motion, it cultivates a mindful, present-centered, and harmonious way of living. If I had to limit my regimen to only two of the hundreds of approaches to self-healing, I would pray, and I would practice Pal Dan Gum.

what is vibrant health?

The healthy body is a flowing, interactive electrodynamic energy field.
Motion is more natural to life than non-motion—things that keep flowing
are inherently good. What interferes with flow will have detrimental effects.
—VALERIE V. HUNT

The notion of vibrant health has been used throughout the book without a full explanation of what this means. Is vibrant health merely the absence of disease, or does it imply the presence of optimal well-being and wholeness of mind, body, and spirit? In order to answer this question, we will explore two energy models of health in addition to the traditional Oriental model. I am referring to the chakra system, developed several thousand years ago, and electromagnetic field theory, which has emerged in this century. Using all three models we will integrate Eastern mysticism and Western science to arrive at a definition that takes into account the energy within the body and the energy field that extends beyond the body.

The human energy field that extends beyond the physical body, invisible to all except spiritually gifted healers, is actually a measurable electrical phenomenon. To those who can see it, it appears as a somewhat egg-shaped cloud of electrically charged particles that hang around the body. This field of energy has variously been called the "aura," "subtle body," "body of light," or "bioplasma;" I will simply refer to it as the "energy body" to distinguish it from the physical body. The energy body is actually an electromagnetic field; that is, it has a charge composed of electrical and magnetic components. This is not groundless speculation, vague mysticism, or New Age nonsense. The existence of an energy body that surrounds the physical body has been verified by contemporary scientists around the world using state-of-the-art bioelectromagnetic instruments and space-age telemetry equipment.

The verification of the energy body is consistent with Einstein's unified field theory—an assumption that combined the understanding of electrical and magnetic fields to infer previously unrecognized electromagnetic fields. Einstein was correct in assuming that all matter is composed of organized patterns of energy characterized by the physical property of electromagnetic force. This sounds complicated. All it means is that everything has an energy field—whether that energy is constellated as a fragrant red rose, your thinking brain, or the book you are now reading. This confirms the most fundamental assumption of Oriental medical philosophy and the foundation of Qi Gong training theory, namely that an invisible energy called Qi exists throughout the universe. The ancient masters were also correct in assuming that the quality of that energy—whether it was strong or weak, excessive or deficient, flowing or blocked—determines our state of health.

Another ancient perspective on human energy fields is the concept of the chakra system. This approach to health, healing, and spirituality appears to have originated in India and found its way into China along with Buddhism. A *chakra* (Sanskrit for "wheel of fire" or "vortex of energy") is an energy center in the human body. According to the ancient Hindu and Taoist healers, these spinning, wheel-like centers receive, store, and transmit energetic information associated with our thoughts, feelings, and experiences. There are seven chakras in all, six ascending along the spinal column and one at the crown of the head. Each chakra is associated with a different endocrine gland, organ system, nerve plexus, emotional issue, and spiritual lesson.

The Taoists integrated the chakra system with acupuncture theory thousands of years ago. They assumed that the chakras connect with the body's acupoints along the twelve main meridians (the Qi channels corresponding to a specific organ, for example, lung, heart, large intestine) and the eight extra-ordinary channels (reservoirs that adjust the flow of energy to the main channels to compensate for excesses or deficiencies). Energy is believed to spin and spiral out from the seven chakras and into the energy field that radiates beyond the physical body. This energy body is a continuous field that extends out from the body at distances that vary with a person's health. For example, when we are feeling good physically, experiencing happiness or love, or feeling spiritually centered and whole, our energy field expands. When we are ill, breathing exhaust fumes while stuck in traffic, or despairing over a life that has become empty or meaningless, our field contracts.

Our bodies are constantly vibrating and each chakra emits energy at a unique and specific vibrational frequency. This is analogous to the different tones that would emanate from individually plucked strings on a hypothetical seven-stringed musical instrument. Ideally, the instrument is in tune, with each string properly adjusted relative to the others so there is agreement in pitch. This means our hypothetical instrument will produce harmonious sounds when the strings are strummed collectively. The same is true for the chakras. When the patterns of energy that emanate from the seven chakras are harmonious and vibrating in proper relation to one another, they are said to be synchronized, or in sync. This is conducive to overall feelings of physical and emotional well-being. Conversely, when the chakras are out of sync, the field is disturbed and illness will result at the site of the disharmonious energy pattern.

Integrating the different models of health (traditional Oriental medicine, the chakra system, and electromagnetic field theory) we arrive at the following definition: *Vibrant health is a condition of balanced and flowing Qi throughout the body's meridians, chakras that are synchronized, and an energy body that is radiant and expansive.* This user-friendly definition is meant to challenge you to go beyond modern medicine's mechanical and chemical theories of health. In light of new evidence from vibrational medicine and consistent with Qi Gong training theory, life is seen as an electrical phenomenon, health a condition of energy in the body, and healing a response to changes in the electromagnetic field. In the framework of this definition, Pal Dan Gum is a sequence of exercises that absolutely *will* improve your energy in the direction of strength and balance.

how does pal dan gum heal?

One of the keys to healing is to view the whole organism as movement.
— Emelie Conrad-Da'oud

If health is defined as free flowing Qi, synchronized chakras, and a radiant energy body, then healing is the body's ability to reestablish vibrant health as needed. *Self-healing takes place as the body uses its energies to restore its genetic memory of wellness. To be healed is to be returned to health by removing obstructions to energy flow and disturbances in the energy field.* These observations hold true whether the field is a cancerous lymph node field, a depressed bone marrow field, or any other field associated with the human organism. They are true whether the field is disturbed due to a common cold virus or a life-threatening AIDS virus. As the energy field improves in terms of strength and harmony, the immune system responds by differentiating self (body cells) from non-self (cancer cells or virus) in order to neutralize the disease agent. If a strong and radiant energy field replaces the disturbed field of the disease, the immune response will succeed and the regeneration of healthy cell tissue will follow.

Let's consider how Qi Gong in general, and Pal Dan Gum in particular, has the potential to heal an illness as serious as cancer. Again, I cannot prove Pal Dan Gum healed my cancer because I was simultaneously praying, meditating, visualizing a healthy lymph system, pursuing loving relationships, and so on. Still, claims of healing various kinds of cancer and other illnesses regularly appear in Qi Gong books and magazines in the Orient. This makes sense when we realize all methods of Qi Gong training are designed to deliver the following three benefits (there are other benefits, but all have these three in common):

- deep relaxation and relief from stress
- deeper and more efficient respiration
- an attitude of positive expectation

Research has shown each of these benefits to be associated with self-healing on a cellular, and even molecular level. This has been established by the field of psychoneuroimmunology, which studies the interaction between body and mind. How this happens is less certain. Perhaps hope and positive expectations activate the process of self-healing, while deep relaxation and proper breathing improve the human energy field.

We know the energy fields inside and outside our body are continually vibrating. Illness results when the body loses its natural vibrational pattern due to the interference of a disturbed pattern caused by abnormal cells or viruses. If a disease agent takes hold in the organism, the body's energies are no longer balanced, free-flowing, and synchronized. This will eventually bring about organ and system malfunctions and the appearance of symptoms—the body's way of informing us it has lost its natural vibrancy. Pal Dan Gum activates the body's innate and natural ability to adapt to a disturbed or "out of sync" energy field. Its gentle stretching movements ensure that the body's energy channels are supplied with an unobstructed and proper flow of energy. This smoothes the flow of Qi in the meridians and synchronizes the chakras to which they are connected.

Pal Dan Gum works according to the principles of acupuncture theory. The integration of movement and meditation regulates the body by adjusting its energies for proper functioning. This is necessary because there are places along each meridian where the Qi becomes easily blocked. These vulnerable places, or points of stagnation, are the body's acupoints. They are both indicators of trouble and sites for treatment. Because they connect with the chakras, blocked or insufficient Qi will throw the energy centers out of sync. The ancient healers adjusted the acupoints by inserting needles (acupuncture) or using finger pressure (acupressure) along the blocked pathway. These techniques release and direct the stagnant Qi and restore a balanced flow of energy throughout the body. Pal Dan Gum is thus like acupuncture without needles, or acupressure without finger pressure. This is not "soft science." The meridian system and the effectiveness of acupuncture and acupressure have been verified by Western medical science using modern research methods.

Exactly how does Pal Dan Gum affect the meridian systems and the flow of Qi to improve health? A metaphor helps to answer this question: Imagine water (or energy) that is flowing freely through the length of a hose (or Qi channel). Assuming there are no blockages, the water will flow without interruption to its proper destination (or bodily organ). However, if the hose becomes constricted, or a kink develops at some point along the way, there will be an excess of water on the source side of the obstruction (resulting in a yang symptom) and a deficiency on the other (resulting in a yin symptom). The point where the obstruction occurs corresponds to the acupoint in need of treatment in order to restore the flow of water. The stretching done while performing Pal Dan Gum treats the obstructed area by elongating the hose. This has the immediate and beneficial effect of removing the troublesome constriction or kink, thus strengthening and balancing the flow of water so it is neither too yin nor too yang. This is how Pal Dan Gum ensures that each meridian will be supplied with an unobstructed and balanced flow of energy, thus nourishing every cell and fiber, every nerve and muscle, every organ and gland, every interacting subsystem in the whole body.

According to Oriental medical philosophy, Qi Gong is both an art and a science. As a science, there is a wealth of experimental evidence documenting its positive effects on the cardiovascular, respiratory, nervous, digestive, and immune systems. As a healing art, it balances yin and yang to give the body abundant and harmonious energy while cultivating a positive and life-affirming attitude. Like other forms of medical Qi Gong, Pal Dan Gum assumes that our energy is inherently health-seeking. The ancient masters recognized the human organism as a naturally self-regulating entity that initiates its own healing, and they discovered that the combination of movement and meditation is a natural way to activate the healing process. This is how Pal Dan Gum heals illness. By ensuring a free flow of Qi, synchronizing the chakras, and expanding the energy body, the physical body is restored to its genetic memory of wellness.

chapter 9

Meditation has to do with opening what is closed in us, balancing what is reactive, and exploring and investigating what is hidden. That is the why of practice. We practice to open, to balance, and to explore.
— Jack Kornfield

Two Qi Gong Meditations For Health And Healing

Meditation, a cornerstone of Oriental medical philosophy for thousands of years, is essentially about awakening our minds and paying attention to what is happening in the here and now. As we have seen, the meditative path is helpful in developing mindfulness and equanimity. These qualities stabilize us in such a way that we become more emotionally responsive and less emotionally reactive—more like the unmoved mountain and less like the active volcano. Meditation is also a way to bring about a proper breathing pattern and a release of tension from the body. It is thus an integral part of our practice because it simultaneously regulates the breath, the body, and the mind. When we meditate, we learn to live in balance and harmony with the world and with ourselves.

Active Qi Gong, such as Pal Dan Gum, is a type of meditation-in-motion designed to get the Qi flowing freely. As we have learned, it uses movement to build and balance the Qi that connects body, mind, and spirit, but is primarily intended to improve the health of the body. The type of meditation primarily intended to improve the health of the mind is called passive Qi Gong. It usually involves sitting silently for the purpose of cultivating tranquillity—a quality of mind characterized by quiet peacefulness and serenity. What distinguishes passive Qi Gong as a type of meditation is that it works with our energy for the purpose of healing the mind and body.

There are many ways to meditate and there are many ways of using Qi Gong principles to enter a meditative state. The ancient Taoist Canon, a collection of more than 1000 volumes, contains hundreds of meditations and healing visualizations. One is reminded of the old story of a man who is climbing a very high mountain. He sees others taking a different path, even going in a different direction. "Fools," he thinks, "They are taking the *wrong* path. They will never reach the top!" He continues what turns out to be a long and difficult climb and eventually reaches his goal. On top of the mountain, he sees the fools who took another path waiting for him. This story underlines the idea that passive Qi Gong is one of many useful ways to enter a meditative state—one that happens to focus on working with energy to balance yin and yang for health. Its goals are similar to other paths in seeking to focus attention, calm the breath, release emotional tension, and maintain inner peace.

The rest of this chapter presents two methods of sitting meditation. Both are elegantly simple ways to practice passive Qi Gong as a complement to your active Pal Dan Gum practice. The first emphasizes proper (Dan Tien) breathing and the second is a healing visualization involving the seven chakras of the human body. Try both and choose the one that feels intuitively right for who you are and what you want to accomplish. The breathing meditation is helpful in improving respiration and the visualization is intended to synchronize your energy centers. Both meditations are excellent for calming the mind and healing the body, but are necessarily brief given this book's focus on active Qi Gong. If you wish to learn more about sitting meditation, there are numerous excellent books on the subject and there is no substitute for instruction from an experienced teacher.

a qi gong meditation for focusing on the dan tien

Choose a quiet place where you are unlikely to be distracted. Sit comfortably on a chair or cushion so that your spine is straight and your feet are grounded to the earth. Allow your eyes to close and draw your attention to the Dan Tien area (about the width of three fingers below your navel and about one-third of the way into your abdominal cavity toward your back). Relax and enjoy this opportunity to breathe properly and rejuvenate your body and mind.

Take a slender and silent inhalation deep into the Dan Tien, pause momentarily, then exhale slowly and thoroughly. Pause momentarily, and take another slender, silent, deep inhalation, pause momentarily, then exhale slowly—and continue with this pattern. Let each breath sink way down into the Dan Tien, your "Center of Vital Energy." If possible, inhale and exhale through your nasal passageways. If you are unable to breathe comfortably through you nostrils, gently purse your lips to ensure that your inhalation is a thin stream of air.

Focus your attention on the *sensations* (not the idea) of your abdomen as it expands and contracts. Practice mindfulness by paying careful attention to any and all sensations in the Dan Tien. When your mind becomes distracted by thoughts or images or whatever, simply return your attention to your breathing pattern (slender-silent-deep) and the sensations of expansion and contraction. In other words, any distraction that draws attention from the sensations of breathing is to be used as a cue to return to the sensations of breathing. Follow these instructions for a period of time (ideally 10 to 20 minutes) and, when you feel ready, open your eyes.

a qi gong meditation to balance and synchronize the chakras

Choose a quiet place where you are unlikely to be distracted. Sit comfortably on a chair or cushion so that your spine is straight and your feet are grounded to the earth. Allow your eyes to close and prepare to focus on your seven chakras, one at a time, with single-pointed attention. Recall that the chakras are wheel-like centers of energy that connect to the meridians and acupoints throughout your body. Each chakra receives, stores, and transmits energetic information as it supplies the vital life force to your cell tissue, organs, and structures. Relax and give yourself the opportunity to improve your energy field by balancing and synchronizing the chakras for vibrant health.

Focus your attention on the first or root chakra located at the base of your spine. Activate the chakra by imagining you are breathing into and out of this focal point. With each breath, visualize a brilliant red ball of energy spinning and spiraling out through the front of your body and into your energy field.

Chakra Centers in the Body

Feel your energy balancing itself perfectly to stimulate your immune system and strengthen your legs and feet.

Focus your attention on the second chakra located at a point between the internal sex organs and the lower abdomen. Activate the chakra by imagining you are breathing into and out of this focal point. With each breath, visualize a brilliant orange ball of energy spinning and spiraling out through the lower abdomen and into your energy field. Feel your energy balancing itself perfectly and revitalizing your sexual organs and bladder.

Focus your attention on the third chakra located at a point just above the navel at the solar plexus. Activate the chakra by imagining you are breathing into and out of this focal point. With each breath, visualize a brilliant yellow ball of energy spinning and spiraling out through the abdomen and into your energy field. Feel your energy balancing itself perfectly and nourishing your stomach, liver, spleen, kidneys, pancreas, adrenal glands, and autonomic nervous system.

Focus your attention on the fourth or heart chakra located at the center of the sternum or breastbone. Activate the chakra by imagining you are breathing into and out of this focal point. With each breath, visualize a brilliant green ball of energy spinning and spiraling out through the front of your chest and into your energy field. Feel your energy balancing itself perfectly and strengthening your shoulders, arms, lungs, heart, and circulatory system.

Focus your attention on the fifth chakra located at the base of the throat. Activate the chakra by imagining you are breathing into and out of this focal point. With each breath, visualize a brilliant blue ball of energy spinning and spiraling out through the throat area and into your energy field. Feel the energy balancing itself perfectly and nourishing the surrounding cell tissue, including your throat, mouth, teeth, and gums.

Focus your attention on the sixth chakra located at a point slightly above and midway between the eyebrows (the "third eye"). Activate the chakra by imagining you are breathing into and out of this focal point. With each breath, visualize a brilliant purple ball of energy spinning and spiraling out through the third eye and into your energy field. Feel the energy balancing itself perfectly and enlivening your eyes, ears, nose, brain, and spinal cord.

Focus your attention on the seventh or crown chakra located at the top of your head. Activate the chakra by imagining you are breathing into and out of this focal point. With each breath, visualize a brilliant violet ball of energy spinning and spiraling out through the crown of your head and into your energy field. Feel the energy balancing itself perfectly, nourishing your musculoskeletal system and skin, and developing your spirit.

A brilliant field of energy now extends out from your physical body and radiates with all the colors of the rainbow. This body of light and color is the natural expression of the Qi that flows throughout your physical body and into your energy field. Each chakra is now individually balanced within itself and synchronized with the other six chakras to make up a complete energy network. Because your chakras are in sync with one another, your body, mind, and spirit form an integrated whole and bless you with personal and spiritual power. Every cell, muscle, organ, and interacting system of your physical body is saturated with the healing power of free flowing energy—the energy of life. Spend some time basking in the warmth and radiance of your healthy energy field and feel it support you throughout the day.

Dear Reader:

My introduction to Pal Dan Gum in 1979 seems nothing less than an act of providence and I've benefited immensely from my daily practice. Writing this book and sharing what I've learned is the best way I know to express my heartfelt gratitude to the ancient masters who originated Pal Dan Gum, as well as those who have passed it along for so many generations. Now I've passed it along to you. Everything you need to know is in the preceding pages—the correct way to execute the movements, how to breathe and stretch properly, what guidelines to follow to ensure success.

Now the ball is in your court. I hope the instructions are clear enough for you to begin your own regular practice. If you do, I'm certain that you too can achieve significant physical, psychological, and spiritual benefits by practicing these simple but powerful exercises. As a meditation-in-motion, Pal Dan Gum offers you a lifelong path of awakening and healing—it is truly a way to vibrant health. Practice well!

Sincerely,

Stan

Stanley D. Wilson, Ph.D.

references

Acharya, P. (1975). *Breath, sleep, the heart, and life*. Clearlake Highlands, CA: The Dawn Horse Press.

Carlson, R., & Shield, B. (Eds.) (1989). *Healers on healing*. New York: P. Putnam's Sons.

Cohen, K. S. (1997). *The way of qigong: the art and science of Chinese energy healing*. New York: Ballantine Books.

Dong, P., & Esser, A.H. (1990). *Chi gong: the ancient Chinese way to health*. New York: Marlowe & Company.

Epstein, M. (1995). *Thoughts without a thinker: psychotherapy from a Buddhist perspective*. New York: Basic Books.

Goldstein, J., & Kornfield, J. (1987). *Seeking the heart of wisdom*. Boston, Mass: Shambhala Publications.

Hanna, T. (1988). *Somatics: reawakening the mind's control of movement, flexibility, and health*. New York: Addison-Wesley Publishing Company.

Hunt, V.V. (1989). *Infinite mind: the science of human vibrations*. Malibu, CA: Malibu Publishing Company.

Jwing-Ming, J. (1988). *The eight pieces of brocade: a wai dan chi kung exercise set*. Jamaica Plain, Mass: YMAA Publication Center.

Jwing-Ming, J. (1989). *The root of Chinese chi kung: the secrets of chi kung training*. Jamaica Plain, Mass: YMAA Publication Center.

Kornfield, J. (1993). *A path with heart: a guide through the perils and promises of spiritual life*. New York: Bantam Books.

Laskow, L. (1992). *Healing with love: a physician's breakthrough mind/body medical guide for healing yourself and others: the art of holoenergetic healing*. New York: Harper Collins.

Le, K. (1996). *The simple path to health: a guide to oriental nutrition and well-being*. Portland, OR: Rudra Press.

Nhat Hanh, T. (1995). *Living Buddha, living Christ*. New York: G. P. Putnam's Sons.

Ni, H. (1994) *Strength from movement: mastering chi*. Santa Monica, CA: Seven Star Communications.

Ni, M. (1996). *The eight treasures*. Santa Monica, CA: Seven Star Communications.

Shih, T.K. (1994). *Qi gong therapy: the Chinese art of healing with energy*. Barrytown, NY: Station Hill Press.

Teeguarden, I. (1978). *Acupressure way of health: jin shin do*. Tokyo: Japan Publications.

Tse, M. (1995). *Qigong for health and vitality*. New York: St. Martin's Griffin.

Tzu, L., translated by Feng, G., & English, J. (1972). *Tao Te Ching*. New York: Random House.

Wang, S., & Liu, J.L. (1994). *Qi gong for health and longevity: the ancient Chinese art of relaxation, meditation, physical fitness*. Tustin, CA: The East Health Development Group.

Wu, Z., & Mao, L. (1992). *Ancient way to keep fit*. Bolinas, CA: Shelter Publications.

Zi, N. (1994). *The art of breathing*. Glendale, CA: Vivi Company.

Stanley Wilson was born in 1944 in Seattle, Washington and raised in the Pacific Northwest. He graduated from Whitman College in Walla Walla, Washington in 1967 with a Bachelor of Arts degree in Psychology and went on to California State University in Los Angeles to complete his Master of Arts in Counseling Psychology. For the next five years, he traveled extensively throughout the United States and Europe, then returned to graduate school to earn his doctorate in Clinical Psychology at the California School of Professional Psychology in Los Angeles.

While working on his doctorate, Dr. Wilson studied for three years at The Center for the Healing Arts in Los Angeles, where he was introduced to the Taoist Physical Arts, including T'ai Chi Chuan. Fascinated by traditional Oriental Medicine, he studied with Iona and Ron Teeguarden at the Acupressure Workshop in Santa Monica, California, where Iona taught him Pal Dan Gum (Eight Silken Movements), an ancient meditation-in-motion and form of Qi Gong (or energy work).

In January of 1980, Dr. Wilson returned to the Pacific Northwest and began private practice in clinical psychology. Several months later, he was diagnosed with a life-threatening illness, and because of its advanced stage, was told he had a maximum of five years to live. This crisis quickened his spiritual development and revitalized his interest in the healing arts. Dr. Wilson attributes his miraculous recovery to the power of prayer and to the extraordinary healing benefits of his twice-daily Pal Dan Gum practice.